Total Speech is accompanied by a number of printable online materials, designed to ensure this resource best supports your professional needs

Go to https://resourcecentre.routledge.com/speechmark and click on the cover of this book

Answer the question prompt using your copy of the book to gain access to the online content.

T0388557

Total Speech

This book explores how speech and language therapists can use a wide range of multi-modal therapy techniques to elicit speech sound. Due to the nature of the approach, there is a limited evidence base in the area, so this book draws on the authors' extensive experience, as well as testimonials from families who have been successfully supported by the approach, to offer a new and unique perspective for therapy. By using a total communication approach, the book provides clinicians with the confidence to be more open and experimental in their practice, when traditional routes are proving unsuccessful, to best meet the needs of clients with more complex clinical backgrounds.

Chapters include the following:

- Setting the scene.
- Persistent speech sound disorders.
- Popular techniques.
- Adding the extra dimension.
- Case studies.
- How to run a Total Speech group.

Total Speech shares success stories of how well-known techniques can be blended to achieve progress and results. It will be a useful addition to any speech and language therapist's therapy toolkit.

Karen Massey has worked as a children's speech therapist in 2 NHS trusts as well as independently, including in special schools, community preschool and Autism Pathway assessments. She has additional training in Oral Placement Therapy, PECS, TEACCH, Signalong and Intensive Interaction. Karen is ADOS trained and has worked within both child and adult autism diagnostic teams. Karen is experienced in working with both high- and low-tech AAC.

Gemma Lester is a specialist speech and language therapist in 3 NHS trusts as well as working independently with special schools, community preschool and Autism Pathway assessments. She has additional training in PECS, epilepsy, TEACCH, AAC, LAMP, BSL and Signalong. Gemma has attended a dysphagia management course as well as Oral Placement Therapy training. Gemma is ADOS trained and is also now working within adult ASD assessment. Gemma is experienced in working with both high- and low-tech AAC.

Total Speech

Blending Techniques in Speech and Language Therapy

Karen Massey and Gemma Lester

Routledge
Taylor & Francis Group

LONDON AND NEW YORK

Designed cover image: ©Getty Images

First published 2023
by Routledge
4 Park Square, Milton Park, Abingdon, Oxon OX14 4RN

and by Routledge
605 Third Avenue, New York, NY 10158

Routledge is an imprint of the Taylor & Francis Group, an informa business

British Library Cataloguing-in-Publication Data
A catalogue record for this book is available from the British Library

ISBN: 978-1-032-37461-1 (hbk)
ISBN: 978-1-032-37462-8 (pbk)
ISBN: 978-1-003-34031-7 (ebk)

DOI: 10.4324/9781003340317

Typeset in Optima
by Apex CoVantage, LLC

Access the Support Material: https://resourcecentre.routledge.com/speechmark

Contents

Acknowledgements

With thanks to all the fabulous children and families who have inspired us through their determination and creativity to overcome numerous obstacles in order to get their voices heard. To their parents, teachers, teaching assistants and siblings who have shared the journey too, allowing us to gain valuable insights and to learn and grow together in our pursuit for speech success with each of the children. Huge thanks also to our own families who have supported us during all the stages of researching and writing, keeping us going and freeing up time to make the task of writing possible. We would like to acknowledge the opportunities to learn and grow clinically through the benefit of working with some incredibly skilled therapy colleagues. We have learned, been challenged, shared special moments and learned some more. Finally, we are grateful to Routledge publishing company for their guidance and collaboration in bringing our ideas and thoughts to print. Without you all, *Total Speech* would not have been possible, so thank you.

About the Authors

Gemma Lester

Gemma Lester is a specialist speech and language therapist, skilled in working with children and young people who have a diagnosis of autism, learning difficulties and complex speech sound disorders. She currently works in independent practice as well as offering support to 2 local charity groups. Gemma is passionate about what she does and she works tirelessly to support her clients' communication in every aspect of life. As an undergraduate, Gemma volunteered in a school for children with severe learning difficulties for nearly 4 years, gaining a wealth of experience of complex speech sound disorders and other learning needs. When she qualified as a therapist she accessed training courses including PECS, intensive interactionand numerous alternative and augmentative communication (AAC) courses enabling her to offer a broad range of interventions to the clients that she works with, always maintaining the stance of 'expecting competency'.

Gemma and Karen have worked together for several years and share many values when it comes to complex speech difficulties. They both resonate with an 'eclectic approach' to therapy, combined with high levels of optimism and belief, as well as the ability to think outside the box. This is what can unlock a child's speech potential.

Gemma lives with her husband Daniel and their wonderful five children Joseph, Thomas, Dexter, Charlotte and Luke. Gemma loves to explore the outdoors with her family and believes they continue to teach her more and more everyday about the beauty of this world. Gemma Lester, Speech and Language Therapist, BA (Hons), BSc (Hons), MRCSLT

www.childspeechtherapist.co.uk

Karen Massey

Karen Massey is a speech and language therapist with a keen interest and specialist skills in the areas of autism and severe speech difficulties involving muscle weakness and muscle coordination. She currently works in independent practice as CEO of All About Speech Therapy Ltd, providing services to children with complex and additional needs online, at home and in school settings. In addition to her training as a speech and language therapist, Karen studied both linguistics and psychology at undergraduate level. She has experience as a teacher working in an East African secondary school and enjoys educating student speech and language therapists within her current practice. Post-graduate training includes PECS level 2, TEACCH, Intensive Interaction and Oral Placement Therapy level 2. Karen has seen from working with children who have a range of complex needs that each child is unique. As such, she places great emphasis on using practice-based evidence (PBE) alongside her knowledge and understanding of each child as a whole drawing from previous experiences and results to shape her practice. She welcomes new ideas and approaches and aims to explore every avenue in order to help children fully achieve their communication potential, particularly if a child is motivated to use his/her own voice. She values the thoughts and opinions of the child as well as family members and education staff as they work together to establish progress.

Karen lives with her partner and their daughter. She enjoys walks in the countryside, reading and spending time with her family.

Karen Massey, Speech and Language Therapist, BA (Hons), BSc (Hons), MRCSLT

allaboutspeechtherapy@outlook.com
https://allaboutspeechtherapy.co.uk/
Twitter @about_speech
Facebook @AllAboutSpeechTherapyLtd
Instagram @AllAboutSpeechTherapy

The Purpose of This Book

It is estimated that around 10% of children have long-term speech, language and communication needs; this is 2 children in every classroom (Bercow: 10 years on). This is a significant amount of children, and it means therapy approaches need to be appropriate and effective in order to make a difference.

Evidence-based practice is the "integration of best research evidence with clinical expertise and patient values" (NHS England). It means that when health professionals make a treatment decision with their patient, they base it on their clinical expertise, the preferences of the patient and the best available evidence.

Speech-language therapists should ideally have access to a sound research base, have a wealth of clinical experience to draw on and also have a good understanding of the patient values. Then they can choose which of these elements is the most important (or a combination of all three) when making clinical decisions for children with speech sound disorders relating to target identification, therapy approaches and the structural or procedural aspects of intervention.

However, the reality is that clinicians often do not have access to all three of these pieces of information. In addition, the perceived pressures of using the 'best research evidence' aspect of evidence-based practice (EBP) can sometimes lead therapists to feel like they should be choosing one therapy technique over another, comparing them and somehow having to rate them or decide which one is better than the other.

Parents who are keen to research and read around their children's difficulties are also likely to draw conclusions that there are 'gold standard' approaches that they should be accessing, again based on general findings rather than their child's specific needs. There is a tendency to over-focus on the 'research evidence' aspect of the above definition of EBP, without considering patient preferences and their own clinical expertise. This can happen leading to 'preferred' therapies being used throughout their clinical practice, or it may mean certain techniques are mapped onto certain clinical caseloads in an administrative exercise, rather than carefully considering each individual case on its own merits. Could it be that some therapies are cheaper and less time-consuming than others?

Then what of clinical knowledge and experience? "Although children with SSD form nearly half a typical paediatric caseload, few are seen by SLTs specialising in child speech disorder" (Pring et al., 2012). This naturally will mean that selection of therapy techniques may not always be well-informed, impacting on the success or otherwise of therapy. Again, the tendency to lean towards any available research may be greater to compensate for any lack of clinical confidence.

Children with more specific speech needs, who are otherwise developing along an age-expected trajectory, might still respond eventually to therapy that is not the optimum. However, children with a wider set of needs, spanning different areas of communication and learning, will fare less well. In addition to this, clinicians can be faced with wider decisions around where to support in therapy when thinking of a child's whole communication system, including skills such as greeting, requesting, following an instruction and taking part in a game. Total Communication can be a very popular term especially when a child's needs are not yet known, or if a child seems to respond to a range of methods. Total Communication can include, although is not restricted to, the use of verbal language, symbols, photos, signs and gesture, voice output technology and objects of reference. So when working with children who are struggling to respond to popular therapy techniques for speech sounds, therapists may decide not to support speech needs. This is why we feel it is so important to share our experiences through writing this book.

The authors have found that, when working with such children, the more methods they added to support speech, the more chances those children had to respond and make progress. The term 'Total Speech' was coined and, in time, inspired this book. If 'Total Speech' were a dictionary entry, it would read something like this:

Total Speech (noun): the act of using a wide range of multi-modal therapy techniques to elicit speech sounds.

As a result of using multiple techniques, or aspects of techniques at any one time, it therefore means that the 'research evidence' mentioned above is unavailable. This is largely due to the fact that it is not possible to separate the individual variables. When research is reviewed, there are a series of 'levels' that indicate to the reader how robust the evidence is. The levels are:

- Level I: evidence from a systematic review of all relevant randomized controlled trials.
- Level II: evidence from a meta-analysis of all relevant randomized controlled trials.
- Level III: evidence from evidence summaries developed from systematic reviews.

Therefore, even at level 1, it would be difficult to establish a 'control group' due to the varying complexities of the children's needs; in addition, due to using a number of therapy techniques, it is difficult to ascribe progress to a particular method. The authors have, on many occasions, sought to find published research relating to speech therapy in children with complex needs; however, minimal studies are available, and the participants' profiles have not been similar enough to the children on our caseloads at the time. Through writing this book, it is hoped that more clinicians might feel confident to be more open and/or experimental in their clinical practice where therapy is not proving successful, in order to best meet the needs of clients with more complex clinical backgrounds.

1 | Speech Sound Disorders – Setting the Scene

So with the known difficulties in gaining clarity from research, where do we start in our quest to finding a system or formula that can adapt to a range of complex speech needs? Let us, first of all, consider what we mean by 'speech sound disorders'. According to the Royal College of Speech and Language Therapists (RCSLT, 2023) in the UK, "speech sound disorders is a term used to cover difficulties that some children have with their articulation, phonological and/or prosodic development". The American Speech Hearing Association (ASHA, 2023) describes it in a similar way: "Speech sound disorders is an umbrella term referring to any difficulty or combination of difficulties with perception, motor production, or phonological representation of speech sounds and speech segments – including phonotactic rules governing permissible speech sound sequences in a language." This means that it is a term covering so many different aspects of speech, and that to really understand the nature of a child's difficulties, we are going to need more information. It is like when you know that a child has a diagnosis of Autism Spectrum Disorder – there are still many unknown factors, such as their level of social interaction, how they communicate with others, how dependent they are upon routines and rituals or how their sensory profile impacts on daily activities. So it is with a speech sound disorder. If someone approaches you to ask, "How can I help a child with a speech sound disorder?" it is going to be necessary to counter with another question or set of questions in order to identify the nature of the problem. We will cover all of the different aspects of speech described in the above definitions within this chapter, from perception through to articulation.

Generally speaking, most children who are native speakers of English master accurate production of all vowels and consonants by age 8 (Dodd

DOI: 10.4324/9781003340317-1

et al., 2003; James, 2001; Smit, 1993a, 1993b; Templin, 1957). Why, then, do some individuals experience difficulties with speech production beyond this age? In 2016, a study by Wren et al. looked at both the prevalence and predictors of persistent speech sound disorder (PSSD). They found that an estimated 3.6% of children will have a PSSD at any given time. These children with PSSD constitute a substantial proportion (8.8%) of clinical caseloads (Broomfield & Dodd, 2004). We will explore the risk factors in Chapter 2. A variety of other terms are also used to describe speech sound disorders including speech delay and speech impairment and, in some cases, verbal dyspraxia (RCSLT). We will talk you through some of the many terms involved in speech sound production, as well as the ways speech can be affected. This will then help us to understand how complex speech really is, and it is not so surprising that some children will struggle to master it all along the way. When we meet parents for the first time, one of the questions we get asked is, "When will my child start talking?" or even, "Will my child ever learn to talk?" It is top of the goals list, the biggest hope and aspiration for many parents. An internet search of early milestones will tell you that a baby's first words are important; it may also tell you that you should be hearing these words by the time your child is 18 months old. So when we meet preverbal children at 2, 3, 4 and beyond, it is not surprising that both the anxiety and the expectations are high. That is long before the age when accurate speech production is typically complete (age 8). The good news for these parents is that there are lots of things that can help. As we identify the specific nature of speech breakdowns, so too can we identify strategies and techniques to support the development of those skills. Thankfully, we do not simply have to wait and see until they are 8 years old whether or not sounds have fallen into place. The rest of this chapter sets out the many different areas of speech that can be affected, including how they impact on speech production. This in turn relates to the Total Speech approach by illustrating just how many aspects of speech we might need to address. Different therapy techniques help to target different areas of speech breakdown, which is why the blended approach to speech enables progress to take place.

Articulation

Articulation refers to "the way in which you pronounce words or produce sounds" (Cambridge Dictionary, 2023). When we speak, we use physiological movements to modify the airflow through our mouth and nose. Each sound can be categorised in 3 ways – the *place* it is articulated, whether or not *voice* is switched on and the *manner* in which it is articulated (Crystal, 1991). This information is often displayed in a chart. Placements for speech include 'bilabial', literally meaning 'two lips'. Bilabial is the placement for the sounds /m/ /b/ and /p/; 'labiodental', involving the lower lip curled back against the upper teeth, is the placement for sounds /f/ and /v/; 'alveolar' where the tongue reaches up to the alveolar ridge – the hard ridge you can feel just behind your top front teeth – is where many of the English sounds are produced; 'velar' – where the back of the tongue reaches up the velum – is the placement for the sounds /k/ and /g/. This is not an exhaustive list, and different languages around the world involve different placements for speech sounds. Voice is controlled by the vocal folds, also known as the vocal cords. When the voice is switched 'on' and the folds vibrate to produce sound, it creates a loud sound; when the vocal folds do not vibrate, we hear what is referred to as a 'voiceless' or quiet sound. For example, the sounds /p/ and /b/ are both produced with the bilabial placement, but /p/ is voiceless and /b/ is voiced. Manner involves the way the sounds are made. This could mean 2 points coming together completely to create a complete stop in airflow (stops or plosives), such as in the sounds /p/ and /b/, or coming almost together to create friction as the air passes through (fricatives), such as in the sounds /f/ and /s/. Stops are relatively short sounds, while fricatives can be produced for a longer duration. Articulation can therefore be affected by difficulties achieving the correct placement, voicing or manner for speech sounds. We have seen a range of articulation difficulties over the years. Three young children who presented for assessment in clinic with articulation difficulties are Archie, Sophie and John. Archie missed out the velar placement for /k/ and /g/ sounds (when the back of the tongue is raised against the velum), so that his production of 'cake' was 'tate' and his 'go' was 'dough', in a process known as 'fronting'. When Sophie replaced her /p/ sound with /b/ and her /t/ sound with /d/, she was struggling to articulate voiceless sounds, using the developmental process known as 'voicing'. And when John produced his /s/ sounds as /d/, meaning 'sock' became 'dock', he was struggling with the manner of his sounds and using the process of 'stopping'. The three examples just described are all typical at different stages in child speech development; whereas there are other speech sound processes that are considered less typical and may indicate more of a speech disorder.

Phonology

Phonology is "the study of sounds in a particular language or in languages generally" (Cambridge Dictionary, 2023). Each language organises and represents its sounds in a slightly different way according to the settings of a small number of features. These are known as 'parameter settings'. The settings create the patterns unique to that language. Settings can include the way stress is used on different syllables, whether or not syllables are CV or CVC, which sounds are permitted to go together and many more. For each parameter, there is a default setting which means the majority of languages will have that setting. An example would be the parameter regarding voice. The language Yidiny has no voiceless consonants, only voiced consonants; whereas there is no language that has only voiceless consonants, as 'voiced' is the default setting for that parameter. Individuals develop their phonological or 'speech sound' system according to the languages they are exposed to when they are babies. Up to the age of 12 months, babies can recognise sounds from all around the world, but by 12 months, they have established their 'home language' settings and dropped the sounds and rules that don't apply. When the individual's system develops differently to the patterns in his or her home language, we might describe this as a phonological or speech sound difficulty. Phonology is a key area of study for student speech and language therapists/pathologists. We learn that the phonological system begins as quite a simple system, with fewer rules, before gradually becoming more refined as sounds are separated and organised with more contrasts. As the process takes place, distinctions between sounds are placed in a developmental order. For example, the distinction between 'voiced' and 'voiceless' sounds is one of the early processes to resolve in English-speaking children; whereas the distinction between 'liquids' and 'glides' involving production of sounds 'l' and 'r' will typically occur much later in development.

Prosody

Prosody refers to "the rhythm and intonation (the way a speaker's voice rises and falls) of language" (Cambridge Dictionary, 2023). Prosody is often one of the earliest aspects of speech that a baby will learn. Singing songs and nursery rhymes help young children to tune in to rhythm and intonation, and many babies will attempt to imitate this pattern long before they are able to understand or repeat the words clearly. But for some children, including those with autism, or verbal dyspraxia, rhythm and intonation is impaired. Their speech may sound jerky, robotic or monotonous – literally 'on one tone'. This can be the case if they have missed out on the babbling stage, where prosody is practised. Altered prosody can affect meaning and lead to misunderstandings, for example, where sarcasm is used. Consider the difference in meaning between A and B below:

A) *I* didn't want carrots (someone else did).
B) I didn't want *carrots* (I wanted something different).

By altering where the stress is placed in a sentence, the whole meaning can be transformed, and by using different intonation patterns, a sentence can be turned from a statement into a question. For example, the phrase 'more carrots' could mean, 'I want more carrots' if said with a falling intonation pattern and emphasis on the word 'more'; whereas it would mean, 'Would you like more carrots?' if the emphasis is on 'carrots' and a fall-rise intonation pattern is used. Even single words can be used to convey a wide range of meanings if stress and intonation is used well.

Speech Delay

Speech delay refers to a delay in the development or use of speech. It can be useful to distinguish between 'speech and 'language before we continue, as we know that as speech and language therapists we sometimes make distinctions that others do not. Speech is the actual process of making sounds. It relates to the physical organs and structures as the lungs, vocal cords, jaw, lips and tongue. So often as therapists, when we refer to 'speech', we are talking about pronunciation; whereas the general population might readily use the term 'speech' to also include expressive language skills such as sentence length and formation. Language delay refers to a delay in the development or use of the knowledge of language, such as vocabulary or sentence length. Speech delay is usually the term we use when a child comes to their appointment and assessment reveals that their speech sound system is immature for their age. An example would be a

4-year-old who has not yet included the sounds expected for their age, as well as later sounds. As a result, people are struggling to understand her when she speaks. See below for details of typical sound development:

Age 4 – what to expect

Earlier Sounds	**m** as in 'mouse'
	b as in 'bed'
	d as in 'door'
	p as in 'pan'
	n as in 'nose'
	t as in 'tea'
	w as in 'wet'
	y as in 'yet'
	h as in 'hat'
Expected Sounds	**f** as in 'far'
	v as in 'van'
	k as in 'kite' or 'car'
	g as in 'girl'
	s as in 'sun'
Later Sounds	**ch** as in 'chair'
	j as in 'jam'
	l as in 'lip'
	r as in 'rat'

When we talk about a 'delay', people often assume this means that at some point, the child in question will 'catch up'. Of course, for many children this is the case, but for others, a 'delay' may mean that they continue to develop skills at a slower rate than their peers, although they still acquire skills in the typical order. It is worth bearing in mind that it can be difficult to predict which children may 'catch up' and which children may have a longer-lasting difficulty. Sometimes when the word 'delay' is originally used, a child's progress may then continue in a less typical pattern. When this is the case, you may more commonly hear the term 'speech disorder' or 'language disorder'.

Speech Impairment

This tends to be a term we hear people use, alongside 'speech impediment'; however, it does not tell us much about the actual nature of the speech. We might still have questions about what exactly is impaired. Does the impairment link to articulation, to place or to manner? Does the impairment refer to the speaker's fluency or voice, and not affect speech sounds at all? An impairment could be very mild, such as occasionally mispronouncing a sound or word, or it could be very significant, where a child is only able to produce a very small number of speech sounds. In 'mild' cases, communication is often successful, and speech can be easily deciphered, whereas in significant cases, a person can struggle to successfully communicate at all, impacting greatly on everyday life. One area we have not considered so far in this book is the relationship between impairment and impact. To the child called Rory who mispronounces only his 'r' sounds, or Sally who has a lisp on her 's' sounds, a seemingly mild impairment might make a huge impact on daily life, whereas another child may mispronounce more sounds yet always be understood. Where fluency is concerned, the way a child thinks about his or her stammer is important to know. We have met many dysfluent children who are happy to persevere until their sentence is out and do not appear to be worried about their speech; and we have met others who have been very frustrated with their speech as well as other people's responses.

Verbal Dyspraxia

> Verbal dyspraxia is a condition where children have difficulty in making and co-ordinating the precise movements needed to produce clear speech with their mouths; and without any signs of damage to nerves or muscles. Verbal dyspraxia is also sometimes called Childhood Apraxia of Speech.
>
> (ICAN)

People living with verbal dyspraxia will often describe great frustration as the messages they want to say are clear up to the point where their mouth has to produce sounds, and they are not able to coordinate their muscles, leading to many misunderstandings. Back in 1997, Shriberg et al. published an estimated prevalence of 1–2 children per 1000, and higher in boys than girls. Although verbal dyspraxia describes a condition specific to speech, it often presents alongside other difficulties in related areas such as language, reading and spelling. Some children with verbal dyspraxia may also have more generalised motor planning difficulties affecting their limbs, known simply as dyspraxia or developmental coordination disorder. The two are not necessarily related, however, and can both exist in isolation. For some children, the difficulties with coordination extend to other oral functions as well as speech, such as being able to pucker their lips to kiss, round their lips to blow bubbles or blow out candles on a birthday cake, to suck up liquid through a straw or to grade their jaw for eating foods with different thicknesses. These additional difficulties are usually described as oral dyspraxia. It is generally accepted that where a child has an oral dyspraxia and not an isolated verbal dypraxia, they are likely to have a longer therapy journey. Progress can take longer and be more effortful. Although verbal dyspraxia is a condition that affects a child's speech, it is often the case that other related areas of development are affected, particularly noted in a school environment. Related difficulties can include, but are not limited to, literacy – phonics, reading and writing – organisational skills, social skills, making friends and general confidence. Recently (at the time of writing), there have been increased efforts within the UK to raise awareness of verbal dyspraxia, as it is recognised that it remains a challenge for both families and clinicians to reach conclusions around diagnosis, as well as the best treatment options. As a result of increased awareness, understanding and guidance, it is likely that the true prevalence rate may be higher than the 0.1–0.2% cited by Shriberg.

Perception

"Speech perception is the process by which the sounds of language are heard, interpreted and understood" (Wikipedia, 2023). Therefore, a child who has difficulties with perception may have associated hearing problems, or perhaps difficulty with active listening when hearing itself is ok. One little girl Karen met when she was just starting out as a therapist was described as having 'ears that heard but a brain that didn't listen'. It was a great description that meant the connection between the ears and the brain was not intact due to auditory neuropathy. Perception takes time to develop as babies and young children make finer distinctions between what they hear. For example, during the first 9 months, a baby will not necessarily interpret any difference between a Japanese speaker and a Polish speaker, yet after this point, more babies and toddlers have tuned into these differences. Difficulties in this area may mean that a child is unaware of their own speech errors, and therefore less likely to spontaneously correct their speech. They may need to spend time building awareness of sound contrasts through listening activities before they begin to alter their speech production. Sometimes children will hear sounds correctly but make errors when it comes to storage. For example, when hearing words with the sound /f/, they may sometimes store the sound as /f/ but at other times store it as /s/, meaning they will then make errors in production as they are unsure which sound to select. We have met a number of children who have this /f/-/s/ confusion, where the word 'fish' may be realised as 'sish' but the word 'swing' may become 'fwing'. In this case, the child has no difficulties physically making either sound, but the errors are due to their perception and storage of the sounds. These perceptual and phonological errors can be described either as consistent (always incorrect) or inconsistent.

Motor Production

Motor speech disorders are a group of speech disorders based on neurological impairment. The differences in nerve function make planning, programming, controlling, coordinating and executing speech very difficult. In terms of understanding this better, it could be likened to when you go to the cash machine and type in your pin: you know the number, but you also know the placement of the numbers – where they are! This is because the brain has laid down a pattern or a program to be followed. In difficulties with motor planning or production, there's a difficulty with the plan that's been laid down or access to it or the body's ability to coordinate the parts of the plan. Have you ever entered a room you visit frequently, only to discover someone has moved something out of place? For example, the bin is in a new location, or the refrigerator door now opens in the other direction? It is surprising how long it takes to relearn the new motor pattern required to successfully throw away your rubbish, or open the door to get some milk! For motor speech, the plan will detail what the jaw, the lips, the tongue, the airways and the vocal folds should do, in what order and how they should coordinate with one another. There is a lot that could go wrong. The plan can fail to be written correctly in the first place; or it can be written correctly, yet difficulties with control and coordination lead to it being executed incorrectly. Incorrect production can then, over time, start to rewrite the plan so that it is stored incorrectly too. For this reason, therapy that aims to help a child achieve accurate production as much as possible – with tactile help as needed – is desirable, rather than allowing a child to incorrectly rehearse a plan that may further entrench errors and make them harder to resolve.

Phonotactic Rules

"Phonotactics is a branch of phonology that deals with restrictions in a language on the permissible combinations of phonemes (2023). Phonotactics defines permissible syllable structure, consonant clusters, and vowel sequences by means of *phonotactical constraints*" (the ability to produce 'syllable shapes' and 'word shapes' such as CV, VC, CVC, CCV, VCC, CCVCC, etc.[C = consonant V = vowel]. (https://educalingo.com/en/dic-en/phonotactic)

Some examples of permissible syllable structures in English:

CV	Bee, no, way
VC	If, on, up
CVC	Sun, pet, house
CCV	Spa, store, sky
VCC	Ask, ink, elf
CCVCC	Spots, bricks, grasp

Phonotactic rules or constraints tell us how syllables can be created in different languages. The rules are highly language-specific. For example, the English words 'star' and 'stop' would not be allowed in Japanese, where /s/ and /t/ are not allowed to join together at the beginning of syllables. Rules are systematic and predictable. Interestingly, even when children have speech errors, their errors will follow the phonotactic rules of the language they are speaking (Dell, 2000). When we consider English, we need to follow phonotactic rules such as 'no syllables may start with /ng/' and 'no syllables can end with /h/'. Some of the rules we have for speaking, such as 'you cannot start a word with /kn/ or /gn/' are different to the way we spell, as in 'knife' and 'gnome', as our words originate from many different languages.

So we have looked at many different ways in which speech can be affected, from the moment sound hits our ears, through to the way we coordinate our mouth muscles and everything in between. When we meet a child and carry out our initial assessment, we will need to know how their speech difficulties fit in with their overall development and presentation. Knowledge of their hearing levels is obviously very important, particularly when we identify difficulties with perception and phonology.

An audiogram shows how different levels of hearing loss impact on the sounds we are able to access. Audiograms are readily available online. When looking at the speech sounds plotted near the banana shape outline, there is no correlation between typical speech sound development and hearing thresholds. Taking just the consonant sounds, 'l' and 'r' are easier to hear yet later to develop in production; in contrast, the sounds 'p' and 'h' are relatively early in production but are harder to hear. This is helpful when meeting a child for assessment because their speech patterns might present very differently if hearing is affected. According to the UK government statistics, 1 or 2 in every 1000 babies is born with a permanent hearing loss in one or both ears.

We will also benefit from understanding how they are finding aspects of literacy, for example, reading, spelling, writing and phonics. Nathan et al. (2004) carried out a study that found children with speech difficulties to be at greater risk for literacy difficulties. Knowing this link exists then, it is important to see how therapy can have wider-reaching benefits that improvements just within the speech domain. When it comes to speech difficulties relating to planning and production, we might wish to explore related conditions such as autism and dyspraxia, as well as physiological differences that can impact on speech production. As we do this, we acknowledge further evidence gaps in, for example, the possible link between ankyloglossia (tongue tie) and speech. Through this further questioning and exploration, we not only develop a much more rounded and holistic view of the children and young people we are there to help, but we can also be much more responsive to changes in their lives. For example, priorities might sometimes mean that communication or speech therapy takes a back seat while a more pressing health need is addressed, while at other times communication might be the biggest priority for them, and therefore speech therapy is an integral part of their support system.

Now that we have covered a range of ways in which speech can be affected, we can think about how we might use the various therapy approaches and techniques to support speech development. We have explored each area of speech above as though it were a discrete area, but as we meet and work with children who have speech difficulties, we soon learn that it is common for a child's speech to be affected in more than one area, thus making both identification of the true problem or break-down more difficult, and selecting the right treatment options more challenging. For many younger children, early identification and input can help them to make gains in their speech, sometimes without the need for direct one-to-one therapy sessions, and their needs will often resolve altogether. However, for a small percentage of children, these speech challenges will persist. This persistence will be the focus of our next chapter.

2 | When Speech Sound Disorders Become Persistent

"Variables identified as predictive of persistent SSD suggest that factors across motor, cognitive, and linguistic processes may place a child at risk" (Wren et al., 2016). In August 2016, Yvonne Wren and colleagues used a Population Cohort Study to look at both the prevalence and predictors of persistent SSD in children who were seen in clinic aged 8 years 6 months. These children were part of the ASLPAC study (see what follows). The final model of risk factors described in the article provides some useful information. It allows us to see which factors might be important to consider and what to look out for when assessing a child in the clinical setting. We might then have a better chance of working out who may be more at risk of developing a persistent SSD.

In a study exploring persistent SSD using data from the Avon Longitudinal Study of Parents and Children – known as the ALSPAC study (Boyd et al., 2012) – the prevalence rate was estimated to be 3.6% of the population. Although we are not able to predict with absolute certainty how each child's speech will continue to develop, the study did come up with a number of risk factors. These factors could prove useful indicators for clinicians, helping to identify children who may benefit from more support as soon as they are identified. The risk factors include the following: at 24 months, only limited examples for putting 2 words together; at 38 months, having limited use of word morphology; at 3 years old, not being understood by strangers or unfamiliar listeners and having difficulty with nonword repetition at school age. Demographic factors also came into play, such as homeownership and gender. Many of the children we have met over our years working in speech therapy settings have persistent SSDs as their difficulties have persisted into school age. As we discuss in many of our case studies and stories, the children have also been working on difficulties in other areas of development, often affecting cognition or learning. This can mean that supporting professionals approach their needs in a different way; it can also mean that their overall profile of strengths and needs changes in response to times of transition, including starting school, or perhaps a hospital admission.

"Children who were unintelligible to strangers at age 3 were 140% more likely to have PSSD at age 8" (McLeod et al., 2012). This is quite long time to spend as unintelligible to others, which we know can increase levels of frustration but also impact on many other areas of development over time, particularly without support.

Sometimes speech difficulties can persist for longer when a child has difficulties across other areas of communication, due to the way that therapy is targeted. Often, clinicians will suggest that therapy should begin where there are gaps at the bottom of the communication pyramid – see Figure 2.1.

As depicted in the image above, typically, we tend to work on skills in this order of the hierarchy; for example, we would support a child's attention

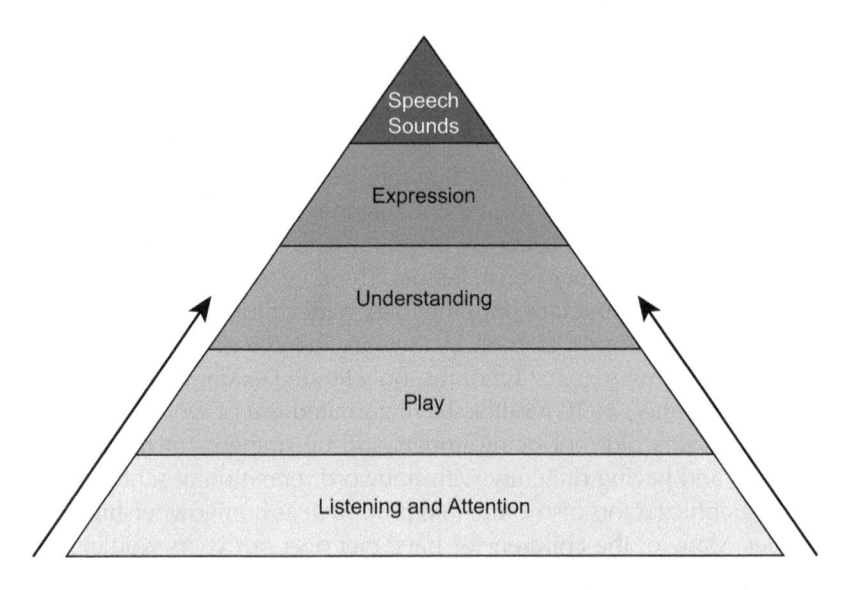

Figure 2.1 Communication pyramid

and listening skills before we would consider working on what might be considered to be higher level skills such as speech sounds. We would help a child to be formulating simple sentences before we would consider finely tuning the building blocks (speech sounds) within these sentences.

As progress is seen in the areas at the bottom of the pyramid, new goals might focus slightly higher up. However, that being said, what happens when we do not target speech sound skills needed to formulate these sentences effectively in the first place? Does a child lose confidence sometimes in being able to effectively communicate with different communication partners if they cannot clearly form words? Do they lose interest in others when those others are not able to respond to their unintelligible word productions? What can actually happen is that the unintelligible child begins to reduce their sentence length as a compensatory measure, in the hope that other people understand what they are saying; they can reduce or stop talking altogether as a result of unsuccessful communication attempts. Moving down to the level of 'understanding', children will often be written off as not understanding language simply because they are not talking, or they are unable to respond verbally to questions and instructions – particularly if they have been offered alternative means of communication to fill the void.

During the preschool years, play is usually easily accessible to most children, with simple interaction such as chase games or taking turns in a physical activity. Younger children also have not developed their awareness of themselves and others to notice when a child is communicating differently. Play is affected when they reach an age where the other children on the playground or in the classroom are all chatting away and games become more sophisticated, requiring some level of conversation to participate. Older children are less forgiving of the child whose speech is unclear, and they may rely more on adult supervision or translation for communication to take place.

When the pyramid is used to prioritise therapy and therapy goals, it can take a long time for speech production to get to the top of the list. By that time, speech errors can become very entrenched, and habits long-standing. If we have a clear indicator of PSSD at 24 months, it could be argued that if that milestone is not met, a child should automatically be referred to speech and language therapy, and intervention should begin straight away in order to help prevent some of the later issues from occurring – adopting a largely preventative approach, but in the light of clear evidence, a child may be at risk of future difficulties. There are two ways of looking at this approach. On the one hand, it would seem an ideal time to offer support, although at the time of writing here in the UK, local services simply do not have the resources to be able to offer such support. At the same time, many other services that have previously worked with families during these early years have also been the victims of funding cutbacks, so that much of the training and attempts at empowering others to deliver early speech and language guidance has been lost. Of course, many children will have continued developing their speech system over this time, and improved social awareness coupled with increased motivation may well lead to progress without ever directly addressing speech. Not everyone would favour the idea of intervening based on a single risk factor that may or may not lead to any future difficulties further down the line, even if resources were readily available. However, there is a group of children who we have met many times over the past few years; this group has not been so lucky with simply 'catching up' over time. So when we begin our focus on speech, we may need to do some 'unlearning' as well as learning new sounds. Imagine someone approaching you to let you know that the way you have been walking for the past however many years is not the way you should walk; and that you need to learn how to walk in a completely different way. To change the way you walk, something that you probably do instinctively and subconsciously, would be incredibly difficult. This is the same for the child who has learned to talk but has been producing sounds with errors and using compensatory placements. A positive side effect of waiting to focus on speech is that older children are often (though not always) more motivated to work on their speech. Their insight may be greater, and they will often really see the value of being able to speak clearly to others. This intrinsic factor can be extremely important.

We also have to sometimes challenge the order in which communication is supposed to develop, due to not all children following the route from attention, through play, understanding and then expressive language. For example, many children we have met who have social communication difficulties or autism may speak long before they demonstrate understanding of other people's language, before they show interest in two-way interaction or see the benefit in listening and attending to other people. They may never 'play' in the ways expected by the developmental textbooks.

So, then, if a child is showing us they have a strength in speech, and they are using it to reach out and make a request, but there are some sound distortions, perhaps it is ok to prioritise their speech clarity? Similarly, a child with significant attention and listening challenges might never be able to fully attend to a prescribed programme of games aimed at improving those skills – perhaps, but not always, linked to hyperactivity or attention deficit or both.

Sometimes it is the way we talk about the pyramid and the interventions we recommend that becomes the problem. For example, when we use Intensive Interaction, a technique that primarily looks at increasing social interactions and gains in listening and attention, we know that we are actually promoting skills at all levels of the communication pyramid, including speech. If we are able to explain this far-reaching nature of the approach, we might find out that parents in particular are more appreciative of our efforts; that we are in fact also working on speech, not waiting to climb up the pyramid one level at a time.

So what can we do to help children who are 'at risk' of a persistent speech sound disorder? Well, let's take each of the 'risk factors' in turn. First, we have the child who, at 24 months old, has only limited examples of putting 2 words together. We can firstly help to boost both expressive language and speech sounds at this point. To support expressive language development, one of the most important things we can do is to model 2-word combinations frequently during play. Setting aside regular 'quiet time' can be very helpful. This involves a time set aside where you reduce all other distractions, you sit down face to face with your child and play together, allowing them to lead. During that time, your role is to observe what they do and join in, wait for them to speak, then recast by expanding their phrases as well as ensuring you are providing accurate speech productions.

Emily's Story

When I met Emily, her daughter Rose had been using single words for some time. At first, this had made Emily really happy, but over time she became concerned that Rose wasn't going to continue making progress – it was always just single words. We looked at different ways to encourage scaffolding from 1 to 2 words. This included adding in some signs. When Rose said 1 word e.g. 'biscuit' we would sign and say 'more' then say 'biscuit' in response. Rose started to pay attention to the sign and started to copy it. Eventually, this led to her copying the word 'more' as well to achieve her first 2 word combination! Emily carried on with this, as well as introducing a 'core words' symbol board. Core words such as 'more' 'not' 'want' 'stop' and 'go' could be added to Rose's single words, using the symbol as an easier route in than just saying the 2 words together. Rose would point to the 'want' symbol then say 'bubbles' and Emily would model 'want bubbles' as she recast the phrase – including the point to the symbol as she did so. This visual support certainly enabled her to 'see' her expressive combinations too. What Rose also experienced via this method was 'positive corrective feedback' where whatever she did say, was then recast back to her how it should be said, with stress being placed on any sounds that may have been difficult for Rose to produce. For example, if she started to say 'doh park' for 'go park' then Emily would agree and say 'yes GO park' – always in agreement with Rose but stressing her speech sound error to help her to pay more attention over time to how this may be said differently. Emily then progressed further using the same techniques until she seemed to naturally extend her language without the additional visual supports.

Symbol Boards and Aided Language Stimulation

Aided language stimulation is a way of supporting children like Rose, who pick up visual information easily. When we think of the number of times a child hears words spoken before they are expected to start using these words themselves, it is often a staggering 21000 words per day. Aided language stimulation aims to expose a child to symbols repeatedly so that they can build their understanding of what each symbol means. This means that when they need to use the symbols, they can do so more confidently. What we have also found is that symbols can be a scaffold for some children who know what they want to say but have not yet developed the spoken words. Through repeated use of the symbol, this then can lead to them saying the word. Even before this happens, the child's communication partner will be modelling the spoken word each time. It works in a similar way to sign supported speech for others. Examples of core word boards can be found on the My Boardmaker and Tobii Dynavox websites. Two popular UK-based systems for sign-supported speech are Makaton and Signalong. Each system introduces key word signing that is always accompanied by the spoken word. Rose responded to both signing and symbols, which made supporting her at this stage relatively easy to implement.

Tim's Story

Tim was another child we met who was still using only single words when he had his second birthday. He had a wide range of words and was using them for lots of different reasons. This meant that he was quite happy getting through the day with minimum effort when it came to communication. His mum, Martha, was worried that he wasn't showing any signs of moving beyond single words. She had tried modelling longer phrases to encourage him, but this had not been working. We sat down and listed the words Tim used already, and we thought about the reasons why he was speaking. We also thought about the different opportunities he was given to speak. Tim was quite an active, inquisitive little boy and he seemed to prefer to do things independently rather than ask for help. This meant that the number of opportunities for communication were reduced, so the first thing Martha began to do was to add some extra barriers within familiar routines. We then thought about some of Tim's favourite things. He was a big fan of snacks and had definite favourites, so this was a good opportunity to teach him that 2-word phrases would help him to get what he really wanted. When it came to crisps, he preferred cheese and onion flavour and disliked salt and vinegar. So Martha placed the crisps inside a cupboard with a new lock. When he asked for 'crisps', instead of giving him the flavour she knew he wanted, she gave him the salt and vinegar flavour, which he then pushed away. This was then repeated until Tim got quite frustrated. When Martha asked him if he wanted 'blue crisps', he attempted the 2-word phrase. For a while, Martha had to work hard at persuading Tim to use phrases in situations where it really made a difference to him getting what he wanted. After some time, this then extended to other situations. After that, whenever Tim appeared to sit back and relax with his language development, Martha knew how to encourage more progress; it usually involved creating more of a reason to communicate and plenty of opportunities throughout the day. In both Emily's and Tim's cases, positive outcomes were achieved by maintaining a strong focus on the end goal of clearer speech. We also see how it is important to adopt a child-led, individualised approach to therapy, so that they were motivated to engage. This meant supporting their existing routes to learning language. For Emily this meant adding in extra visual supports, whereas Tim only needed auditory input with the increased need to communicate clearly.

Next, we can look at word morphology at 38 months. Word morphology relates to the extra parts we add to the beginning or the end of words to alter their meaning slightly. For example, break versus break*ing,* can versus can*'t,* book versus book*s.* One of the earliest examples of word morphology is adding -ing to the end of a verb to describe what is happening. So if Charlie says 'Daddy eat chips' instead of 'Daddy eating chips' or even 'Daddy's eating chips', he is missing this word morphology and may benefit from adults taking time to model the use of -ing when it's relevant throughout the day. Of course, not all word morphology is expected to be present in all 38 month olds, but -ing, regular plural -s, use of the article 'a' are some early morphemes to look out for. The plural -s can be particularly challenging for children who are later to acquire the sound /s/, so it is worth checking if this sound is even possible for them to produce before aiming to have this plural marker in their speech.

Rayyan's Story

When Rayyan reached 3 years old and was not being understood by strangers or unfamiliar listeners, his mum realised that it was starting to have an impact on how he was coping on his nursery days. At home, she was an expert in reading his non-verbal signals and could anticipate most of his needs. She also realised that she was 'tuning in' to his particular speech patterns (which is wonderful when you are their main care provider, but as we know, the older our children get, the broader the range of adults and children they encounter). This made it hard for a long time to see that there could be a problem. Maybe it was everyone else? Were they just not listening or giving him their full attention? When it was clear that this was not the case, she agreed it was best to make sure that she was supporting his communication in the same ways as nursery. This included attending a signing course so that adults could sign to Rayyan, and he could use some signs to communicate in return. They also took lots of photographs and used visuals to help others understand what he was saying when his speech was unclear. At nursery, they included a lot of listening activities and fun ways to practise making different sounds too and early concepts, such as loud, quiet, fast and slow, which is essential in being able to recognise particular sounds (for example a /d/ is essentially a louder version of a /t/). This was something that all the children benefited from, not just Rayyan. A huge benefit to this was that people started to focus more on the messages being communicated rather than how Rayyan was speaking. His mum felt much more relaxed about things. When people around you relax, you also become more relaxed, which is the perfect environment for communication to develop naturally. This is what happened to Rayyan, and he continued to make progress with his speech to the point where he was much more intelligible, and adults gradually faded out the additional support as it was no longer needed.

Jayden's Story

We met Jayden when he was 3 years old, and his mum Lanie got in touch because she had noticed his speech wasn't very clear and knew that if it didn't improve, he would be at risk later in wider areas, particularly self-esteem. She had tried reaching out for support through local services, but due to long waiting times, she realised that she needed help sooner rather than later, so I met her as an independent therapist. Through talking to Lanie, it quickly became clear that she really knew her son well, and despite not being a trained speech therapist, she had worked out that his speech did not have a clear pattern, and errors were inconsistent. He attended a day nursery 3 days per week, where the staff adored him, but there was no additional focus on speech, so his needs were overlooked. At home, Lanie often found herself 'translating' for other family members who struggled to understand Jayden much of the time. Jayden was a very bright little boy who demonstrated excellent understanding of language, and he was also keen to express his many ideas in full sentences. This made his speech errors stand out further, and I could see the frustration in his face when his messages were not understood first time round. Lanie worried that over time he would lose confidence and opt out of social situations. Through play and books, we were able to gather a large sample of Jayden's speech and found he did indeed have an inconsistent speech pattern. Lanie was soon equipped with the tools to support his speech development at home, while at the same time continuing to respond positively to what he said rather than how he said it, ensuring she capitalised on every opportunity to boost his confidence and self-esteem in other ways. Using a core vocabulary approach and Cued Articulation, she reported progress in less than a week with some words. This motivated both Lanie and Jayden to continue in a positive light. Through continued support using this approach, Jayden reached a point when he had been at school a year, and everyone could understand him. In fact, people who met him at that point would never guess he had previously struggled to speak clearly.

This particular risk factor is a very common reason for speech therapy referrals, whether by parents or nurseries. Considering how important we now know this is in the prediction for future persistent SSD, local policy does not always offer much comfort to parents of preschoolers with this concern. As independent practitioners, we are fortunate to be in the position of offering support at the point of referral, allowing us to confirm any speech sound difficulties and offer the early intervention that can make a difference. Whilst we acknowledge that not all of these children who present at age 3 will go on to develop longer-term speech needs, we are not able to predict exactly which ones will and which will not, therefore we can not only help to reduce child frustrations through improved clarity but also parental anxiety through support and reassurance that help is available and their concerns are being heard.

David's Story

When David was in the reception class at school, he found talking to people a challenge. He still had a lot of speech errors, and even though he really wanted to contribute in class, to chat to the other children and make friends, they often didn't understand him. David was referred to his local speech and language therapy service, and he attended clinic for his appointments. After several therapy sessions, David's progress was minimal, and he lacked confidence with tasks that required thinking about the sounds and working out what he could hear, as well as just producing the correct sounds in words. In other words, his phonological system appeared to be the point of breakdown rather than presenting with an articulation difficulty. A conversation with his teacher revealed that David was also finding some of the phonics and literacy activities more difficult than most of his peers. As a result, we decided to explore his phonological awareness skills, including his ability to repeat real words and nonwords (made up words). David had much greater difficulty copying the nonwords compared to the real words. This coincided with one of the predictors for SSD, and David went on to receive therapy for his speech until the end of year 1. He also accessed small group sessions in school to support his reading. David was able to make good progress with the right support, and this meant that he could achieve clearer speech as well as support within the classroom for literacy when he needed it.

Lucy's Story

Lucy also found nonword repetition particularly difficult, and it was felt to be a factor in her long therapy journey towards clearer speech. She appeared to have difficulty with motor planning as well as difficulties retaining the sound string for long enough to repeat it accurately (phonological memory). Just like David, Lucy needed support in school for early reading and writing in addition to her speech therapy sessions. Later on, when speech therapy was no longer indicated, Lucy continued to have some challenges with language, for example, her vocabulary knowledge appeared lower than that of her peers, perhaps due to difficulties storing new words. However nonword repetition affects a child – with speech, vocabulary or literacy – it remains one of the key risk factors for persistent SSD, so seeking support is worthwhile.

When considering these risk factors, we also need to understand what is the impact. If a child goes on to have these residual speech errors, what happens? Research has shown that children with persistent speech errors face an increased risk of social challenges such as the ability to make friends and to effectively communicate with them, emotional challenges such as having insufficient means to express their emotions and the emotional impact on development when you cannot express yourself effectively. As therapists, we have had the privilege of having front row seats when it comes to this, as both the challenges have played out, and children have started to lost their social confidence; but equally and importantly, we have seen the positive knock-on effects socially as children gain speech clarity, which is quite wonderful to see.

We also know that there are academic challenges such as difficulties developing literacy skills, as cited by Snowling and Stackhouse, which underpins their entire school day. Previous research has also shown that the effects of speech sound disorder may also then persist into adulthood and span multiple domains of activity limitations and/or participation restrictions, as defined by the World Health Organization's International Classification of Functioning, Disability and Health (ICF) model.

So we have explored the key predictors for an SSD becoming a persistent SSD, including some of the children we have met who have presented with these predictors. We have shared how we approached therapy, and described their therapy journeys. In the next chapter, we are going to look more closely at some of the most popular therapy techniques used to help children with speech sound development. You will notice that many of these techniques use auditory and visual methods.

3 | Popular Therapy Techniques

When it comes to therapy techniques or approaches for children with speech sound difficulties, there are many to choose from. Some are more widely used than others, and clinicians may adopt preferred techniques for a number of reasons. Sometimes it is due to adherence to the current evidence base, or to local clinical care pathways, and other times it is down to the level of familiarity and experience with the approaches. However desirable the requirements are to provide both an effective and efficient intervention, we are aware of the practical shortcomings. We will now discuss a number of the therapy techniques commonly used by clinicians. How many have you heard of? Are there any reasons you might or might not be tempted to find out more about some of these techniques? Perhaps you could add another dimension to your therapy toolkit. After all, we are all learning as clinicians and sometimes we discover new and exciting approaches that can really transform our therapy success.

Core Vocabulary Therapy

Core vocabulary therapy involves using a list of highly motivating words that are personal to the child, then practising those words repeatedly. Through repetition, it is hoped that pronunciation will improve. This happens naturally in typical development, so using this as an approach makes a lot of sense. For this approach to have maximum impact, it is important to consider the sound make-up of the words included, ensuring they are sounds and strings or sounds that are achievable based on

DOI: 10.4324/9781003340317-3

the child's starting point. For example, if you know a child can already produce the sounds /t/, /d/ and /b/, then choosing 'teddy' and 'table' would be sensible words; however, 'chocolate' may not be so easy to achieve if you have not already heard /ch/, /k/ or /l/ sounds before. This therapy technique is particularly popular for children who have an inconsistent phonological disorder – they say the same word differently on different occasions, and it is hard to identify a 'pattern' to their speech. Toby (who I first met when he was 4 years old – an energetic boy who always showed an interest in interaction) used this approach in therapy, and he engaged really well; and because the words were so meaningful to him, it meant that he practiced them several times a week beyond the therapy sessions too. Over time, as the focused words grew clearer and more consistent, his overall speech system also gained consistency, and the organisation of sounds in his brain appeared to improve, leading in turn to the better production of new words.

Dynamic Temporal and Tactile Cueing (DTTC)

This motor learning approach to therapy is one of the recommended approaches for children with apraxia of speech (CAS) or verbal dyspraxia. Dr Edythe Strand is one of the key proponents of this approach, and she has often used it with children who have very severe CAS, are still preverbal and may have unsuccessfully accessed other types of therapy. One of the big differences between this approach and others is where the focus goes during therapy. DTTC talks a lot about the movement between sounds during speech, rather than just building the sounds themselves. The rationale for this focus is that CAS is a result of difficulties with muscle planning and muscle movement. Another key aspect of this therapy is the use of 'the principles of motor learning', which Strand argues is essential to helping children with CAS. The implementation of this therapy approach takes the child through a number of levels of difficulty, beginning with direct imitation of natural speech. This, of course, is incredibly difficult for the group of children who struggle to imitate speech – hence why DTTC may be considered; however, it is the level that they will then work towards during therapy. If this direct imitation is not possible, then the child and the therapist will speak at the same time, prolonging the vowels in the words. For example, the word 'box' would be pronounced as 'booooooox' with a much longer medial vowel sound. As the child is producing the vowel, the therapist can monitor their mouth stability, such as jaw positioning and grading, or lip movements. When production is accurate with the long vowel, then gradually the length of the vowel would decrease until the child is able to produce the word accurately alongside the therapist at a typical rate. However, we still need to get to the point where the child can speak clearly without the support of someone else, so DTTC then involves the adult gradually reducing their volume as the child maintains theirs. The ability to follow the instruction to continue speaking without also reducing volume to a mime is key for success at this stage – this may not always be easy. Then the aim is for the child to imitate speech directly after the adult, then with a slight delay, before ultimately achieving spontaneous speech. By breaking down the process into the different stages, it is easy to see how you can step up or step down therapy in order to meet the child exactly where they are during a therapy session, responding in the moment. DTTC relies on the use of a range of cues, including auditory, visual and tactile. For example, with a child who has struggled to move through the different range of vowel sounds, saying the words together and elongating the vowel, he was able to achieve this more successfully).

Metaphon

Metaphon was developed by Dean & Howell in 1986 and is based on the principle that homophony motivates phonemic change. You would begin by screening a child's speech sounds to gain a profile of what they can produce and what errors they are making. This would enable identification of the phonological processes they are using.

Metaphon ultimately aims to help children develop and use metalinguistic awareness when it comes to speech. Often, visual resources (i.e. symbols that may represent concept within sounds such as long/short/loud/quiet are taught in meaningful tasks. Through exposure to these symbols, they gain meaning). These aspects are introduced explicitly to help children who are able to think about how they are talking. The concepts are accompanied by pictures, such as a person shouting to represent 'loud', and a person placing their finger on their lips for 'quiet'. An example where Metaphon might be used is when a CVC (consonant + vowel + consonant) structure may lack the final consonant sound each time, in which case the child's awareness would be drawn to the end of the word. Visual resources might use the carriages of a train, with the end carriage missing in the child's production but present when the adult models the correct production. When Tilly came for therapy, she was 'stopping' many sounds, for example, /s/ became /d/ (so the word 'sun' would be produced as 'dun' by Tilly), and /f/ became /b/ (so the word 'fish' would be produced as 'bish' by Tilly). This typical speech sound process has a huge impact on intelligibility (i.e. Tilly was very difficult to understand if you did not know the context). Using Metaphon during therapy, she began to think about the sounds as either 'long' – /s, f/ or 'short' – /d, b/. This helped her to both hear the difference between the sounds before she started to produce the 'long' sounds herself.

Metaphonetic skills are worked on to improve a child's 'cognitive awareness' of the properties of the sound system, while metalinguistic tasks are used to develop more successful use of repair strategies which, in the long term, enables a child to 'own' their speech capabilities.

Phoneme Awareness Therapy

Phoneme awareness, or phonological awareness, describes a set of pre-reading skills that typically develop during the preschool years, although children may not have the ability to talk about the skills until they are slightly older. Children become aware that words are made up of a series of individual sounds. They start to recognise and identify letters they see and sounds that they hear, making the link between them. They gain skills that will become crucial for speaking, reading and writing. Phonological awareness skills include rhyming, alliteration, segmenting words into sounds, combining separate sounds into words – also known as blending – and understanding that there is a link between the sounds in words and their corresponding written letters.

Most people who are familiar with an Early Years curriculum will know that phonological awareness tends to form a big part of the current teaching for early literacy skills. Popular approaches, including Jolly Phonics or Read Write Inc., use phonological awareness skills within their delivery. The phonics approach focuses on learning the individual letters and sounds before starting to combine them to form words. Just as we can use these skills for reading and spelling, they are also applicable to speech. Although a large proportion of our clinical caseloads have included visual learners, who have begun reading through what is known as the 'whole word' approach, it is easy to see how phonics skills or phonological awareness skills are beneficial alongside this so that children can work out how to read or say new words; otherwise every single new word would need to be learned separately, which would be an incredibly big task! When a child has difficulties in the area of phonological awareness, they will often make speech errors as well as finding reading and writing particularly difficult. Conversations with others involved in a child's learning are really useful to understand the full extent of their difficulties and come up with a joined up approach where possible.

The Psycholinguistic Framework

The Psycholinguistic Framework (Stackhouse & Wells, 1997) is a model used by speech and language therapists to investigate the underlying nature of children's speech, language and/or literacy difficulties and target intervention accordingly. It is highly specific, is taught during speech and language therapy training programmes and is widely used as a means to understand how speech works. It can be considered the marmite of the SLT world as it can provide highly detailed analytical information regarding someone's speech and language profile while being torture to get your head around (particularly as a student).

How Does It Work?

Whilst traditional speech therapy may consider solely the child's output of speech and language (e.g. working on the production of correct articulation of speech sounds), this model also takes into consideration the organisation of sounds and words within the child's linguistic system; for example, has the child stored the word or speech sound correctly? Is the child hearing the difference between certain speech sounds? In a nutshell, it determines which of the following areas are affected (or multiple areas at a time).

The speech processing model depicted subsequently, based on Stackhouse and Wells' (1997) psycholinguistic model, takes into account speech development, word finding skills, phonological awareness and literacy skills.

In order to better understand this model, it is helpful to consider an example, starting at the first box in the model and taking the word 'cat'. Information about this word will be stored within a person's vocabulary (lexicon) as follows:

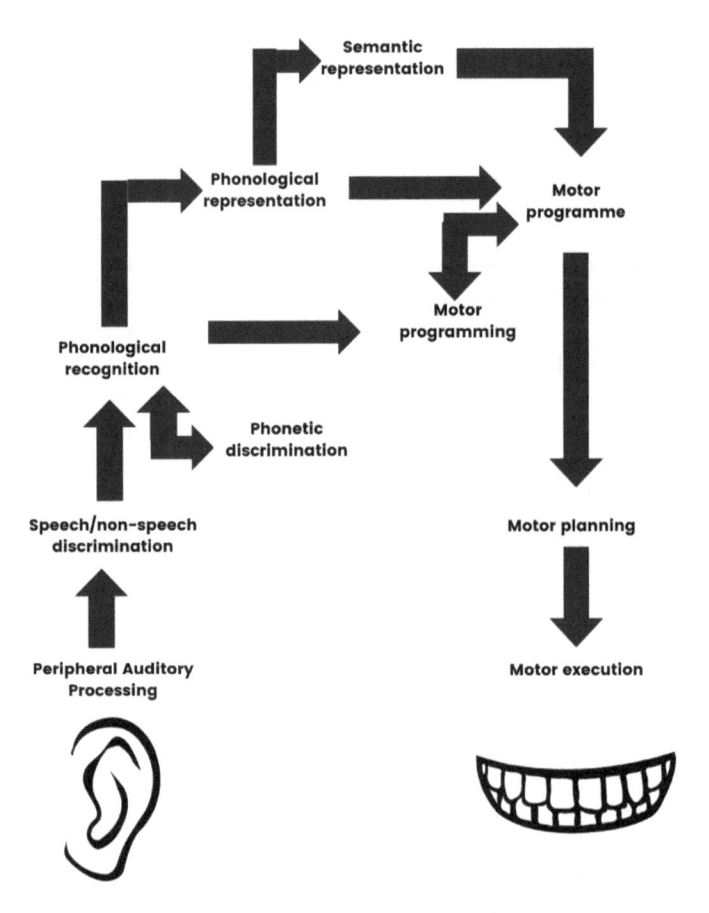

Figure 3.1 The psycholinguistic speech processing model

Semantic representation – Knowing what the word 'cat' means (e.g. it's a pet, it's furry, it has 4 legs and a long tail).

Phonological representation – Identifying the word 'cat' from auditory (hearing) and visual (e.g. lip reading) cues and discriminating it from similar words such as 'cot' or 'hat'.

Motor program – Knowing how to say the word 'cat' and not having to think about it every time it is produced.

Grammatical representation – Knowing how to use the word 'cat' in a sentence (e.g. 'the cat is drinking milk' or 'we bought a cat yesterday').

Orthographic representation – Knowing how to spell 'cat' and understanding it when it is written down.

The following screening assessment can be helpful in this 'unpicking' where the difficulty may exist if it is not obvious from a child's speech output (what we actually hear):

INPUT:

Does the child have adequate hearing?
Can the child discriminate between speech sounds in nonwords?
Does the child have language-specific representations of word structures?
Can the child discriminate between real words?
Can the child demonstrate auditory discrimination through picture selection?
Is the child able to detect rhyme?

Speech and language therapists working within the psycholinguistic framework will therefore use activities (as in the profile above) aimed at tapping into specific areas of the child's linguistic system in order to identify areas of difficulty. Intervention targets are then set and worked on accordingly, using the child's existing strengths as a foundation for therapy, working through the model from input towards output.

Similarly, if the difficulty appears to lie in a child's speech output, it can be profiled and analysed using the following:

OUTPUT:

Can the child access accurate motor programs for naming?
Can the child manipulate phonological units to create rhyming words?

Can the child repeat real words with clear articulation?
Can the child repeat nonwords?
Does the child have adequate oral motor skills to produce sounds?

Traditional Articulation Therapy

The traditional articulation approach is one of the most well-known and widely used interventions. It is extremely popular as an initial therapy that you encounter when learning your craft as an SLT. It was developed by Van Riper in 1978. With this approach, the SLT (speech and language therapist) works on one sound at a time in a logical manner and progresses from working on the sound in isolation, later syllables, moving into words and eventually phrases, sentences, reading and conversation. The diagram below can be helpful in explaining this hierarchy or steps often referred to as the 'steps to learning a sound'. This is usually a fantastic way to show parents the upcoming trajectory of their child's speech development journey:

This is not ideal for all clients and is optimised when used with younger children with a few sound errors as they are still developing language skills. In addition, this approach can also be used to correct the articulation errors that are relatively developmental in nature.

You can summarise the Stages in the Traditional Therapy Approach in the following way.

The speech-language therapist selects one sound at a time for the child to work on (let's say /k/). The SLT has to follow a certain logical flow of stages in order to utilize the traditional therapy approach, with an achievable increment at each level. The first step is working on the single sound /k/ in isolation by playing certain listening activities or with hand signs. Then the child will work on the sound /k/ at syllable level. For instance, if you are working on the sound /k/, at this stage you may practice 'key', 'cow' or 'yuck'.

The third stage is working on the sound at the word level. For instance, you may work on 'come' or 'cat'. This stage will also include the sound in various positions, meaning the initial, medial, or final, that is, 'cat', 'maker', and 'book'.

The fourth stage starts to feel like real progress and is where the success can start to snowball if effective, and you would work on the sound at phrase level, like 'your cat'. Towards the end of the intervention you have carried out, at stage 5, the child will practice the sound at sentence level,

Steps in learning a new sound

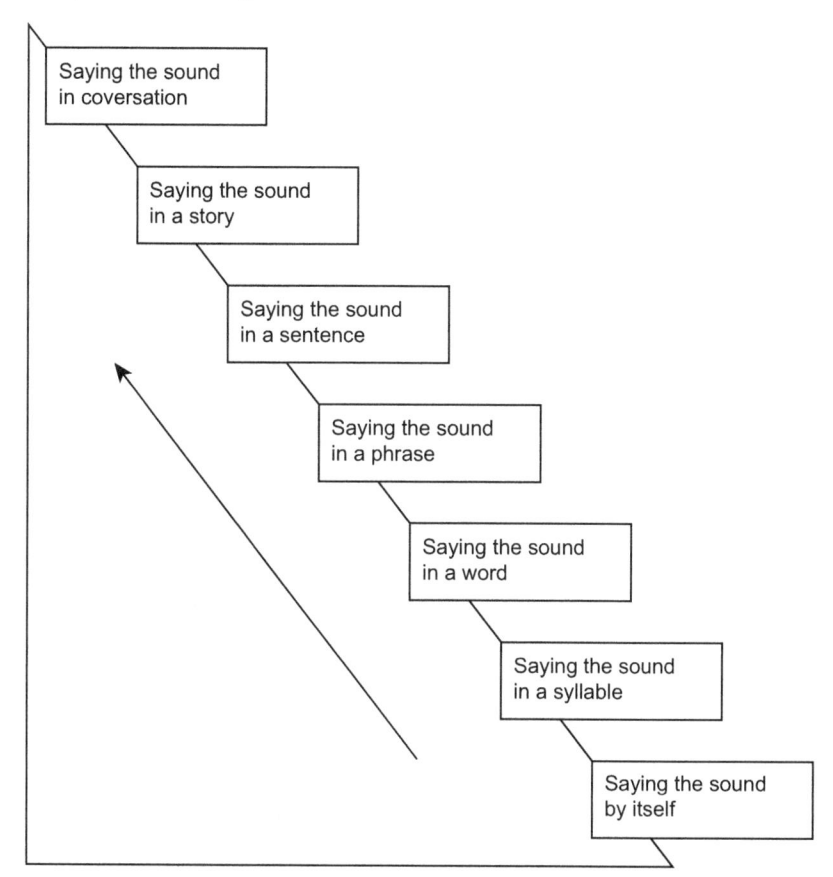

Figure 3.2 Steps involved in speech sound clarity

for example, 'I cooked a cake, and Kerry kept cool'. The last stage is to work on the sound in everyday contexts of conversation. This can be more challenging to see in terms of generalisation; however, tongue twisters are fabulous at this point to consolidate all the hard work:

A cupcake cook in a cupcake cook's cap cooks cupcakes. Cool clams cleared the cave. Cook pumpkin pancakes for breakfast.

This approach also forms the basis of the Nuffield Dyspraxia Programme, which builds sounds from single sounds into words in a predictable way. Words are gradually expanded in both length and complexity, with a focus on multiple repetitions within therapy sessions. When starting out in the speech therapy world, we had a handout showing the 'steps to speech sounds'. It was a really useful visual showing how speech sounds progress from the individual sound on the bottom step, all the way through to sentences on the top step (we would need to request permission to insert a visual here from the Nuffield Dyspraxia Programme). Usually, once a child has begun their journey with a particular sound climbing the steps, they will continue to make progress until they reach that top step. Sometimes, like in Patrick's case, only the first couple of steps need to be explicitly taught before a child will fly up the rest of the steps and off into conversation without a backwards glance; other times, like for Alice, the journey of individual speech therapy sessions is much longer, as each step is carefully negotiated then rehearsed, over and over, before cautiously stepping out into everyday conversation with confidence. Occasionally, as with the physical steps, a child may stumble and fall down a few steps along the way. Usually this happens if practice is inconsistent, focus is not maintained or they are struggling to build on several speech sounds at the same time. Working out what to do to rectify the situation will then help them to get backup and make progress once more. If you find that you are supporting a child's speech in this way but they get 'stuck' at the steps you practice within therapy and cannot seem to take their new speech skills beyond the therapy session, it might be the case that they have broader difficulties with executive functioning and not just a straightforward speech sound difficulty. Explicitly teaching and supporting the generalisation of sounds within a range of everyday situations and activities will then be necessary. You would also likely find that these difficulties with generalisation are not limited to speech work but can also be found in the child's progress with reading, literacy and mathematics. Support from an educational psychologist may be helpful at this point.

Auditory Input Therapies

Auditory input therapies involve a child listening to multiple repetitions of a sound – sometimes referred to as 'bombardment' – with no expectation that the child should copy or say the sound. Sometimes this approach involves listening through headphones to increase attention for the sound or sounds being presented. This may be particularly useful for children who struggle to listen and focus on speech within a busier environment. The low demands involved mean it is usually well-tolerated by children who may otherwise find it difficult to engage in direct therapy tasks. For example, when Sally first came for therapy, she would sit quietly and deliberately not speak when it was her turn during games as she was aware she had a speech problem and was too shy to practise in front of anyone. However, with auditory bombardment, there was no pressure on her to speak, so she felt much more relaxed. This kind of therapy improved her awareness of specific sounds as well as her understanding of associated words and word structures (the storage part of the Stackhouse and Wells model described previously). After some time using this approach, Sally began to take active part during therapy as she said words out loud in tandem with the words she was hearing.

Minimal Pairs

In phonology, minimal pairs are pairs of words or phrases in a particular language, spoken or signed, that differ in only one phonological element, such as a phoneme, toneme or chroneme, and have distinct meanings. They are used to demonstrate that two sounds are two separate phonemes in the language; for example, at the end of a word, it might look like 'row' and 'road'. At the beginning of a word, this might look like 'mile' and 'smile'.

Why do we use them in speech therapy? They are the perfect way to give a child a physical consequence for an inaccurate pronunciation of a word. They can be used in therapy to help children learn that swapping one sound can change the meaning of a word. It brings meaning to their error.

It may be easier for the child if minimal pair pictures are presented to them so that the meaning of the word is clear. They can be used to help correct a range of speech processes including final consonant deletion, initial consonant deletion, fronting and backing, stopping and gliding.

Maximal Pairs

So if minimal pairs consist of 2 words closely matched but differing only by one phoneme just one step away, maximal pairs are designed to contrast two words but with a much more obvious phonemic difference. For example, instead of *tea* and *key*, which has a slight change in placement, *tea* and *bee* offers more contrast due to the change in both placement and voicing, or *bee* and *see* differ in both placement, voicing and manner (a 'stop' versus a 'fricative'). When engaging in therapy tasks, it is unlikely that the child will confuse the two words for each other in maximal pairs, but there is a greater focus on listening and organising words beginning with the initial sounds and expanding the child's sound system accordingly.

Cycles Therapy

What is cycles therapy? The cycles approach treats children who use a lot of different phonological processes (error patterns) by targeting each process for a short amount of time and then 'cycling' through other phonological processes:

For example, for a child who needs support to develop fricatives (f, v, s, z) as well as velars (k, g), you would present 'f' and 'v' for one cycle (or perhaps a terms worth of input). Then you would cycle on to your velars for one cycle of input. At the time you revisit your initial sound, you may find it has now consolidated in production. Therapy is continued for each process until it is eliminated from the child's conversational speech.

This approach is popular for many reasons. This includes the relatively short time involved in delivering the therapy sessions. It is also helpful as it is really clear at any point which sound is the focus; for example, now we are working on the sound 'd'. However, there are potential downsides to the approach for children who experience memory difficulties. When the focus on a particular sound is over, there can be a long time before it comes around again in the cycle, by which time, previous progress may have been forgotten. This is quite typical of children with moderate learning difficulties where they need a very high level of repetition when learning new skills before information is transferred from the short-term memory into their long-term memory.

Cued Articulation

Cued Articulation essentially is a system that considered using hand signs in order to show a child or person how we articulate a sound in the mouth, where it would otherwise be difficult to visually see. It considers a colour-coding system that also uses single and double lines to represent whether or not voice is used. This is separate to other types of signing, and the value of using signs and visual support at speech sound level helps the child to learn what the sounds are, whereabouts in the mouth they are made, how they are made, that they are different, that they have meaning, that they can be represented by symbols and that they could be strung together to make words. Each sound has a different cue which can be

Figure 3.3 How to produce sounds /m/ and /n/ with finger and voice clues

shown as a picture to help you know what to do. Where a picture has two lines next to the mouth, it indicates the sound is made with voice switched on, whereas one line indicates the sound is voiceless. The lines then translate into your fingers when you are making the sign – one finger for voiceless and two for voiced. For details of all the cues, we recommend Jane Passy's book (2010), *Cued Articulation – Consonants and Vowels*. We mention this method again in Chapter 8 as part of our Total Speech pathway.

All of these therapy techniques are widely used in clinical settings to support children with a range of developmental speech difficulties. They predominantly use auditory and visual methods, and in the majority of cases, they will be enough to make the difference, helping children to make progress and graduate from therapy with clearer speech. We too began by adopting many of these methods in our own clinical work; however, we became frustrated when things did not work, when progress appeared to plateau or stop; and we became increasingly curious as to whether or not there were other options out there yet to explore.

4 | Adding an Extra Dimension

For most children, most of the time, the excellent approaches discussed in the previous chapter are enough. Speech therapy for a very specific difficulty such as a speech sound disorder has a good chance of working. We both use many of these methods too.

What we notice is that popular approaches tend to rely on the use of auditory and visual cues, that is, saying something and showing something to encourage a child to copy a sound. In our work with children who have more complex needs, including a range of learning difficulties, autism spectrum disorder and Down syndrome, we often have to draw on extra tools from our toolkits. We have to research and trial new ideas. Sometimes these new ideas and approaches have limited appearances in the evidence base, something that we are acutely aware of. The thing is, children with a complex set of needs are not usually represented in research, so it is difficult to apply evidence to practice in these cases. When trawling the evidence base to decide how to support a group of children with different complex needs with their specific phonological difficulties, we found only a small number of studies that had focused on children with Down syndrome, who also had a degree of learning difficulty. The evidence base for speech therapy in general is often lacking in robust studies that can be reliably used to inform therapy; but when you are working with children and young people with a learning disability, that evidence base shrinks further still. It is compounded by the fact that any research paper that would get to the stage where it is taken seriously would have to look at just one therapy technique at a time, otherwise it would not be possible to identify what was responsible for any progress seen; yet we would very rarely choose to use only one therapy technique at a time. Typically, even for children who are responding well to auditory methods, we would still employ 2 or 3 different auditory methods to help them.

One of the things we are able to do in our roles is to consider adding in an extra element or dimension to therapy. It is through considering an extra element to therapy we are inclusive to those children that learn differently. We not only use auditory and visual input but we often add in an extra sensory or tactile input too. This helps children to actually feel what to do with their mouths when they are struggling to imitate or respond to 'say this' and 'copy this' instructions. We have seen these adaptations within the classroom as teachers within a specialist classroom will often add in multi-sensory materials to teach concepts from maths to science to history. Our colleagues in physiotherapy or occupational therapy will also choose to add tactile approaches to aid different movements or positions within their work. We have observed and worked with teachers for children with different sensory impairments or loss, as well as music therapists and art therapists. All working with the same groups of children and all embracing the multi-sensory way of working.

To help illustrate this way of working and how we have made our decisions regarding therapeutic input, we will talk you through some real-life cases, where we have met children needing differing levels of input. As you will read, each child is different to the next; and it is less about their clinical diagnosis or needs, and more about how they respond. As a result, the exact collection of tools in each child's speech toolkit is likely to be very bespoke to them, and may not necessarily be successful for the next child, even with the same clinical description of need.

1) ***Jonathan – a case where a child needed to just listen and tune in more to be able to improve speech clarity – what we did and how it worked.***

When 10-year-old Jonathan entered the clinic room with his mother one Friday morning, he came with a clear goal in mind. It was only 2 months until his older brother got married, and Jonathan had been asked to prepare a speech! He really wanted to improve his speech clarity so that the other wedding guests would hear what he had to say. His mother explained how something had been 'switched on' inside his head, and she felt that he was now really motivated to put in the effort required to make progress. She was also thinking ahead to high school and said it would be brilliant if he could start there without his speech difficulties as she knew it would be important for his confidence in a new school. Jonathan explained how he had attended therapy when he was younger but stopped when he was about 6. His mother added that Jonathan had gotten fed up with having to attend the appointments, showed no interest in working on his speech and had improved enough that he could get by ok in school. However, the 10-year-old boy who arrived in clinic that day was really quite self-conscious and had started to ask why his speech was still different to his mates. Jonathan found the following sounds difficult to produce: sh as in *sh*op, ch as in *ch*op and j as in *j*ump. We got straight to work, and Jonathan was quickly able to tune in to his problem sounds. He could hear the difference between correct and incorrect productions and was aware that his own productions were not the same as the target sounds. He went away after the first session with the task of achieving the sounds in isolation in a consistent manner – there was no structural reason why he could not achieve them, and when he experimented with his placement, he could occasionally achieve the right sounds. Jonathan returned the following week ready to move onto whole words. Again, determined to succeed, by the end of the session, he was able to accurately produce all 3 sounds in words consistently. Off he went with a slight spring in his step to continue his practice! His mother said that he had been practising in front of the mirror each evening. By the end of the 8th therapy appointment, Jonathan was able to speak much more clearly. He was rehearsing his speech for the wedding and could self-correct during conversation when he noticed his speech slipping. His story is an example of how an older child, with a high level of awareness, plenty of motivation and a clear goal, could improve his speech significantly in a short space of time, with mainly auditory input alongside some practice in front of the mirror. Jonathan did return to clinic one final time. He was pleased to report that he had successfully delivered his speech at the wedding, and the smile on his face spread from ear to ear!

2) ***Max – a younger child who also needed to tune in and listen more to his own speech in order to improve clarity and intelligibility for others.***

Sometimes we have met children nearer the end of their speech therapy journey, like Max. Max had already attended many therapy sessions, and his speech sound system was almost complete. During therapy sessions, Max no longer made any errors, even when we worked on full sentence production. He was given the 'all clear', and off he went. But his teacher noticed that she didn't always 'catch' what he was saying. This was the same for his peers and for family members he spoke to over the telephone. When we explored this with Max, we found that he had stopped thinking about his speech, assuming that he no longer had any needs in this area. He was a very enthusiastic boy and was often rushing to tell some exciting news or get to the next best activity in his day! When we sat down and had the conversation about his speech, he joined in to create a plan for improving his speech. The majority of the plan involved awareness. By consciously listening to his own speech, slowing down his rate of speech and learning to self-correct his errors, he was able to quite quickly become more intelligible to others in school and at home, even during conversation when excited or tired. These additional factors – such as our emotional state, how tired we are, as well as our environment – contribute to the intelligibility of all speakers, whether we have speech sound errors or not, so having the ability to identify them and make adjustments can make a real difference.

3) *Katie – a case where a child benefited from lots of visuals added in to therapy, then they 'got' it.*

I remember Katie as a little girl who loved to sit and watch other people. She was a very observant child and would spot straight away if someone in class had a haircut or new shoes! Katie always paid attention to the front of the class when her teacher was talking, telling a story or showing the pupils how to do something. But although she looked like she was listening, she often forgot what had been said shortly after she heard it. She had what is known as auditory processing disorder (APD). This means that she struggled to listen in noisy environments, to follow instructions, to maintain her attention and to locate sounds. Katie also had some speech sound difficulties that impacted on her ability to communicate with her friends. Her teacher discovered that she was more likely to remember information if she could see it. So we explored different visual ways to support communication in the classroom, including signing. Katie also responded well to whole word reading approaches and could recognise the letters in the alphabet when she saw them. Progress with speech had been very slow, and Katie knew she was not doing very well with the listening and attention games we repeated on a regular basis. So we added in more of a visual approach to therapy. We made sure that we always paired spoken sounds and words with pictures and text. We highlighted and underlined 'tricky' sounds so that they stood out more to Katie when she saw them. We added Cued Articulation to help her see which sounds were expected when we practised words, and sitting side by side in front of the mirror meant that Katie could watch our mouths together and try really hard to copy. By adding in these extra visuals to therapy, Katie began to make progress again. Her confidence improved when she realised that she could be better understood by others, including her friends.

4) *Joel – a case where a child needed to see the word structure in longer words before he could say them clearly.*

Joel had mastered all of the sounds needed for speech, and he was very good at producing short words, but when faced with words that had 3 or more syllables, he would shorten them, so that 2 syllables collapsed into one. When he tried to imitate someone saying the word, although he would listen, he repeated the word back in his own version. It seemed that he had already stored the words incorrectly and was not aware that he was repeating the words differently. So we thought about how we could help him to 'see' the difference. We drew pairs of words on paper in two columns. The first column showed the word with all its syllables, and the second column showed Joel's shortened version. Straight away he could see how they looked different. We then helped Joel to understand that words have different numbers of syllables by separating the syllables on the page and counting them together. Finally, we clapped each syllable as we read it out loud. To begin with, Joel would read out the words one syllable at a time, pointing to keep track. Then gradually, he was able to switch to reading the words as he clapped along. After many successful repetitions, Joel challenged himself to say the words without looking to see if they had 'stuck' in his memory. This method worked, and every time Joel encountered a new long word, he would write it down and visualise the number of syllables before he learned how to say it correctly.

5) *Ciaron – a case where a child needed tactile input on top of the other methods before they began to achieve certain sounds or placement.*

Ciaron was quick to use PODD mats to communicate his daily requests but found it much harder to understand how to articulate speech sounds. He started off by doing simple kissing sounds in games with his mum, and this quickly developed into a 'p' followed by 'b'; however, achieving the other consonants and the different vowels was much trickier for him. We knew he needed to develop a broader range of vowel sounds, otherwise the amount of functional words he could start to use would remain very restricted, and this is where a tactile approach became really useful.

Ciaron started to copy the 'ah' sound, and this was helped by him looking in the mirror, giving him the feedback as to what his lips needed to do. It was harder for him to see what the other vowels looked like (as they are not as visual), so we chose another visually different one in the 'ee' sound. We would gently help his cheeks to fall back into that wide smile position and hold them there until his lips started to achieve this, reducing the tactile prompt as we went along. One of his favourite books was *That's Not My Bee* – as you can imagine, this gave us lots of opportunity to repeat and practise this sound in a fun context.

A tactile approach again was needed to help him to achieve the 'oo' sound, shaping his lips forward and round. We used this approach alongside the mirror, bubbles and a little straw piece cut off at the end to help the lips really achieve that lip rounding while he blew the bubbles. Mum would also look for as many opportunities to do blowing activities across the day to really give him that experience of putting his lips into those different and contrasting positions. Some of the children we have met have not liked the bubble mixture, so a similar activity has worked where, instead of blowing a bubble, the child blows into a straw with a ball that hovers as a result, or they blow air throw a round mouthpiece to inflate a small balloon.

6) *Taylor – a child who also needed to listen, see and feel what to do in order to achieve speech sounds.*

When we first started working on Taylor's speech, he tended to use some vowels with a 'd' or occasional 'g' for variety. Aged 4, he was able to recognise many letters of the alphabet and could identify which sound adults were producing by pointing to a choice of 4 letters, with 100% accuracy. We decided to add visual support to speech work and began our focus on the bilabial (lips) sounds 'p', b' and 'm'. Taylor learned to copy the Jolly Phonics actions that went with the pictures and songs, he mastered the Cued Articulation signs for the 3 target sounds and had a particular interest in all things *Peppa Pig* and bubbles, and yet the bilabial sounds continued to elude him. Taylor knew what was expected but could only get so far as placing his lips together before he switched to a 'd' sound instead. Other sounds gradually emerged, and we eventually parked the elusive lip sounds in despair. Then one day, 3 years later, a conversation took place about the use of shapes to provide visual and tactile input for sounds. Using 3 different coloured shapes – a triangle to represent 'p', a square to represent 'm' and a circle to represent 'b' – in less than a week, Taylor learned to produce the sounds! It was quite remarkable to see his achievements after so many attempts that had not worked. The 'apraxia shapes' were what he needed to really feel the sounds, even though he could hear and see how the sounds were produced. Apraxia shapes are discussed in more detail in Chapter 8 as we take you through Total Speech – the pathway.

7) **Jake – a child who had used visuals for a long time to communicate but who showed a real interest in vocalisations**.

When we started working on Jake's speech, he had successfully used a range of non-verbal methods including PECS, PODD and choice boards. Jake would often watch his mum's mouth during moments of intensive interaction and was keen to imitate her movements but would 'grope' often to try to find the accurate position. Again, we started on those visual lip sounds like 'p' and 'b' and 'm'. We used a combination of things like the facial massager to alert the facial muscles in the first place. We then added in a chewy tube to help the jaw to become more stable. Apraxia shapes then gave his lips that physical 'information' about what to do. We usually used them in conjunction with the bite tube hierarchy, straw and horn hierarchies (see https://talktools.com/pages/resource-library).

He would also feel his mum's mouth when she made the particular sounds which he was able to tune into. He loved to do this in songs too and imitate the song.

As he started to broaden the range of consonants he could make, we were able to introduce vowels. This was never done in isolation from visuals and instead was always backed up with Nuffield dyspraxia pictures. This meant that Jake started to build his knowledge of what each Nuffield picture meant and, through consequence, they became more and more meaningful the more frequently they were used.

We also utilised Jake's thirst for structure and order (e.g. if we had set aside 10 sounds to practice, Jake would need to finish all 10 before he wanted to end the activity). We were able to increase the number of speech reductions he was able to do, which meant his progress accelerated very quickly.

As well as ensuring that we view each child with a unique lens, to ensure we build up the right package of therapy that will help them achieve their communication – including speech – potential, we also adopt a clear method for working out how many sensory layers to use. For example, we do not simply jump straight in with a full multi-sensory approach that uses tactile methods in the first instance. We would begin with more traditional methods using auditory and visual input to see if the child responds positively. If they do, then we would fill their toolkit with this kind of input only. However, if it is clear they are not able to respond to this input, at this point, we would trial tactile methods to allow them to feel what their mouth is doing. We add extra layers as needed. Equally, when therapy has been progressing well and specific sounds are achieved, we naturally peel away the layers that are no longer needed, beginning with the tactile layer, progressing to visual and finishing with auditory supports or reminders until speech skills are generalised. Having access to this logical progression of supports has really enhanced our ability to offer the right therapy options at the right time. It has reduced frustrations when children have reached points where progression has appeared to stop, and it has answered so many previously unanswered questions about the exact nature of the child's difficulties as well as what we can do on a practical level to overcome them. Parents have many times found the explanation that goes alongside this way of working to be clear and easy to digest. Many times they will say that they can see their child knows what they want to say, but there appears to be some physical reason why they are unable to do so. Having physical supports to tackle physical problems therefore makes absolute sense.

Let us talk for a moment at this point about intelligibility and what it means. There can be a tendency for us all to think more about the child whose speech is not yet clear than their conversation partner. A child's speech is rated on a scale from intelligible to unintelligible, and therefore, if their speech is unintelligible, they need therapy to improve and become more intelligible. It is something that we all might do, clinician, parent, teacher or otherwise. However, have you thought about all the other factors that come into play when it comes to how intelligible someone's speech might be? It actually can vary greatly from one environment to another and from one listener to another. When we tune into the other variables, we realise that there is actually a much bigger picture and many other areas that could – and perhaps should – be of focus that we can often adjust more easily and more quickly than a child can make progress with speech sound production.

Listener familiarity is a common factor in intelligibility rating. If you know the child well and spend lots of time in their company, you are likely to 'tune in' to their speech and thus rate them as a clearer speaker than an unfamiliar counterpart. Therefore, spending time and getting to know a child better could be one way to help in the case of a child with speech sound difficulties.

Next, we can consider the environment in a general sense – how busy is the room? Is it noisy or quiet? Are there any competing background noises such as music, screens, equipment? Is the window open or closed? Are there lots of visual distractions that might affect our focus on the child who is talking? Having the optimum environment for listening with minimal distractions and being able to focus on listening to the child can make a big difference. We can also think about positioning – are we close enough and face to face so that we can use lip reading cues to help us? Do we need to adjust our level so that we are not too high up? This too can help.

Knowing the subject matter is another thing that can make a difference. If we are familiar with the topic of conversation, then we are more likely to be able to understand and interpret what we hear, compared to an unfamiliar topic. When faced with a child chatting away about their favourite video game, for example, Karen has often struggled to understand due to the unfamiliar vocabulary and terminology, yet when conversation has switched to everyday activities, suddenly speech has seemed clearer. Finally, we know that when we are in a two-way conversation, we tend to mirror our conversation partner. This means that if a child is speaking fast or quietly, we as adults can model a slower rate of speech and a good volume, and then the child is likely to also slow down and speak at a louder volume.

So now we can consider how much time we spend not just providing the child with all the direct therapy techniques and support they require but also on educating the key adults within their environment on adaptations they too can make to help verbal communication be as successful as possible along the way to clear speech.

What starts out as a seemingly straightforward area of the speech and language profession can in fact become incredibly complex with many, many facets. This is why we began to explore the patterns and the routes through the path from preverbal to verbal for the children we have met with more areas of need than most; the children who can too easily get forgotten when it comes to prioritising lists that are just too long. There is never a sure-fire, foolproof plan, but in the next chapter, we share how we have used out toolkits to help different children gain their voices.

5 | Time for Total Speech

So what can we do as clinicians when a child has spent years in therapy with little gain in speech clarity? What if all that focus on speech using auditory and visual techniques did not work? What if we have tried a tactile approach instead, but it is not leading to the positive change we had hoped for? This is when it is time for Total Speech. This simply means using every tool we can find within our therapy toolkits to support and promote speech. It means working with all aspects of the speech model, from hearing, through processing and understanding, then programming, placement and production. It means working with our colleagues in related areas such as sensory occupational therapy and physiotherapy. It also means learning from what works in different aspects of a child's life, through observation and discussion with teaching staff and family members who know them best. Children with complex needs often benefit from a wider range of supports, incorporating multi-sensory approaches with more physical and sensory help, rather than following one specific programme or therapy package. This is the way they learn lots of things, from how to move their limbs during physiotherapy, to writing their name or placing an empty cup in the sink. To communicate in other ways, they may benefit from hand over hand support to make the hand shapes needed for signing, to exchange pictures during Picture Exchange Communication System (PECS) or to find the right page in an AAC app. So for speech, we should then expect to have to support them in similar ways, allowing them to hear, see and feel what speech is about. Through regular discussions with our colleagues from physiotherapy and occupational therapy backgrounds, we have often been met with the assumption that how we are working – using tactile inputs to support auditory and visual methods – is what these children need for their speech to develop. They have offered their own work as examples of how this makes sense to them. They have equally wondered why more emphasis is not made of the value these tactile approaches can have. We, of course, know the complexities within the research and evidence base for speech and language therapy, as well as the voice of popular opinion among many in our field. It is the progress and success in front of us that has persuaded us to persevere with what has worked in spite of these challenges. So let's share some more of these stories that are based on real-life clinical cases.

Meet Carl. Carl was a 12-year-old young man with a diagnosis of ASD. He was preverbal but a great communicator in many other ways. He competently used PECS and Proloquo2go when opportunities were presented in familiar situations. He would also seek out adult interaction many times throughout the day. During these times, he would become very vocal and appeared desperate to use his voice. He rejected the familiar symbol-based communication systems on offer, as though they were not quite enough. Something else people noticed with Carl – he would reach out to touch your face and throat as you were talking, seeming to feel what was happening, trying to understand how it worked. At times previous therapists had wondered if Carl might have features of a verbal dyspraxia; however, with no repertoire of speech, it was not possible to confirm this, and he did not respond to therapy at the time aiming to teach him speech sounds using visual and verbal approaches. We decided to start from the beginning and assess Carl's oral motor skills. During the assessment, we found no muscle weakness – so dysarthria was not the problem – but we did find out that Carl loved sensory input to his mouth. He would request it repeatedly by reaching out and bringing the beanbag or the facial massager back to his face, and he would break out in a broad grin each time. After a lot of sensory input, he began to hum, which gradually became the sound /m/. With regular practice, Carl worked out the motor plan to make the sound /m/ with more and more precision and less effort. It was very exciting – and also unexpected – to see at the time! Carl really enjoyed his therapy sessions. They were times he really looked forward to them as part of his week in school, and he appeared to gain much benefit, not just from his new-found skills in creating speech sounds with his own voice, but his confidence and happiness generally would extend to before and after the sessions, carrying him into other lessons in a positive light. He gained positive feedback from others each time he showed off his new skills, and the teaching team working with him at the time helped to identify words that he might aim to use; words that would be both functional as well as achievable based on the small number of sounds he was beginning to master. This team approach was key to ensuring that Carl was supported to practise his speech throughout the week.

Next, please meet Eliza. Eliza was a 7-year-old girl who had attended her local clinic for therapy since she was 3. As a 3-year-old, she had presented with many of the predictors for a persistent SSD. She was not combining words age 2 and was unintelligible to strangers age 3 1/2. She also had a history of glue ear, which had affected her hearing until she had grommets. Prior to meeting Eliza, she had received therapy to help with early language development. This had gone well, and the focus had shifted to address her many speech sound errors. In school, her speech difficulties impacted on literacy, confidence and friendships. Progress in therapy had slowed down, and by age 7, she appeared 'stuck' on some remaining sounds. Her regular therapist expressed frustration at the lack of progress; the frustration was naturally shared among Eliza and her mother too. When Eliza's case was brought to my attention, it was noted how the remaining difficulties centred around tongue placement. A couple of questions for her mother, and we agreed that tongue placement and movement was key to her residual problems as well as further progress. We discovered that Eliza was not yet able to hold her tongue in either the elevated position at her alveolar ridge (necessary for clear production of sounds such as /n/, /t/, /d/, /l/), or in the depressed position behind her bottom teeth with the back raised to the velum (needed for clear production of the sounds /k/ and /g/). This meant that she was also struggling to establish a consistent placement for the sound /s/. We quickly set to work on the oral placement programmes needed to address this. She enjoyed the challenge of holding cereal up to her alveolar ridge for as long as she could, with the mirror to help her self-monitor, and the adults in the room for competition! She was also able to begin the similar programme holding the cereal down behind her bottom teeth as she got in position for /k/ and /g/. After a few weeks of regular practice, she was able to start alternating these two placements, and finally even her /s/ sound was produced more clearly. It was not a magical 'quick fix' as Eliza did have to continue daily practice for several weeks. However, she, her mum and her regular therapist expressed relief at finally having a clear explanation for her difficulties, a clear plan to follow and tangible progress each week as a result.

Then there was Jake. A fabulous young man who received a diagnosis of autism at the age of 5. Jake always showed a strong desire to communicate (again, he was already effectively using PECS and communication books); but he had a reduced range of consonants and vowels that he used effectively as words. He found speech so challenging and would often become frustrated and upset for such long periods that it would upset the kilter of his entire day when not understood.

Using a combination of techniques including apraxia shapes, Talk Tools and Nuffield dyspraxia articulograms, Jake started to pay more and more attention to his own mouth and his mother's mouth during speech sound practice. What started off just with Jake being able to produce simple words that began with /g/, he then started to include more lip sounds (p, b, m), which quickly then built up into short words like 'iPad' and 'open', and he has just learnt how to shake his head for no. His family were in complete disbelief at how quickly the speech started to come, and his school then started to offer opportunities across the day to practice these core words more. So often, we have to work to help a child have that initial speech success before others around them sit up and take notice. It just takes one or two people to believe in the possibility that speech *can* come, for it to happen and to transform that child or young person's life. The changes in self-esteem and confidence can be both instant and long-term when they realise that they have the ability to overcome such a huge barrier and struggle and begin to use their own voice to communicate successfully with others.

Sometimes a combination of the right tools and the right timing comes into play. It certainly did with Francis. This young man was keen to connect from a young age. He would approach newcomers enthusiastically with a thumbs up, he waved hello and goodbye and at 4 he could say 'Mama' in context. He revealed that he had taught himself to read, so began using text and symbols to improve the messages he sent to others. Out came the speech tools from the speech toolkit. Everything was trialled in a bid to help Francis use the voice he was craving to use. But sadly there was no progress, despite the motivation of all involved. Francis continued to use text, symbols and also signing as systems to support his communication. He continued to say 'Mama' and was vocal in every other way but speech.

Then a year after the speech tools were placed carefully but sadly back in their box, Francis was introduced to a voice output communication aid (VOCA). He was so excited to find a voice in the aid and delighted in chatting to others about so many things – where he had been at the weekend, what he enjoyed doing and asking questions about time (a topic of particular interest to this day). Then one day, Francis began using more sounds. It started with the initial sounds in words to name important people in his life at the time. Just the initial sounds, but by pointing at the person as he said the sound, it was clear who he was talking about. It was a very exciting moment! Something had clicked. The dots were joining up, and Francis was finally ready to begin his speech journey. He took very gratefully and enthusiastically to the Nuffield Dyspraxia Programme, and in a few short months, he was saying many, many full words. His vocabulary soared, and once he started, he was determined to use his own voice, replacing the voca that had given him a big stepping stone along the way to finding his voice. It wasn't long before he was participating fully in school lessons using his voice as his preferred communication means, with symbols very much as a back-up system, or when he wanted to tell a big story.

When Brendan used the sound /g/ for every verbal attempt, he was introduced to pictures for sounds at the beginning of the Nuffield Dyspraxia Programme – see Chapter 8 for more details of this programme. Details of how this programme is structured will be discussed in the next chapter, under the heading, 'Targets That Focus on Different Word Structures'. This visual approach allowed him to demonstrate his ability to learn and understand the different sounds when spoken by other people. If someone said one of the sounds, he could scan and select the right picture. Brendan tried hard to start producing more single sounds, with daily practice in school and at home with the sound cards from the programme. When he had a small number of single sounds that he could produce accurately, the second stage of the programme was introduced to help him blend 2 sounds together to make CV (consonant-vowel) and VC (vowel-consonant) combinations. At the same time, more single sounds remained a goal. While he was able to bring his lips together to use /m/, /p/ and /b/, he found it very difficult to elevate his tongue tip to achieve the placement for alveolar sounds. This is where the tongue tip touches the alveolar ridge (the bony ridge behind your top teeth), which is the placement for many of the English consonants. Despite much effort by all involved, Brendan did not manage to gain this placement through auditory and visual methods alone. So he began to follow the Talk Tools ™ programme for tongue tip elevation. In the original programme, a cheerio is used, but Brendan's preferred food for this therapy was barbecue flavoured Pringles! A small piece of crisp was broken off and placed onto his alveolar ridge for him to find with his tongue tip. This helped him to have a tactile reference as to where he needed to place his tongue. It worked, and when he was able to hold his tongue in place for long enough and use muscle memory to repeatedly achieve the placement, the sounds that had been missing were gradually produced.

Brendan's story is one that we have seen repeated through many children. A recent success story is that of Phillip. Phillip's speech journey began in a very similar way, although only the vowel sounds were being used. Like Brendan, the desire to communicate was there, and he could use a high-tech voice output communication aid (VOCA) to communicate his basic needs effectively. The desire to be a verbal communicator was very clear, and together with dedicated parent involvement plus a therapy assistant who believed in the end goal, after just 6 months, Phillip made clear progress. His progress was specific to the therapy tasks implemented daily. They included both Oral Placement Therapy and the Nuffield Dyspraxia Programme. After a year of this input, more people began to take notice and comment on Phillip's progress. The child who had previously relied solely on his VOCA to communicate in school was beginning to show off his voice there too, demonstrating a clear wish to talk instead of using his device all the time. What we know is that all the support we can offer to help a child's communication skills, no matter which kind of communication method, will go some way to helping a child get one step closer to speech. What we also know is that just because a child may have achieved effective communication skills in one of those alternative communication methods does not mean they should not also be given the chance to use their own voice for speech, either as well as or instead of AAC; particularly if that is their wish to do so.

Wesley presented himself as a candidate for therapy as he was determined to be a verbal communicator despite reaching the age of 13 and not yet speaking. For most of his primary school years, Wesley had spent much of his days seeking comfort in his specialist interest activities and both seeking and avoiding all the sensory information at his disposal. With such intense interests and sensory needs, he really didn't have the time and energy left for communication. He was encouraged to access and use PECS at a basic level but only engaged reluctantly to get his basic wants and needs met. Wesley's academic abilities were not rated highly, and he attended a school for children with severe learning difficulties. So when he began to use a high-tech communication app and one day he composed his request to learn to speak, everyone was shocked, not least his own family! By opening up his access to a much wider vocabulary, Wesley finally had a system that he could use to communicate what he really wanted to say. He did have another challenge that would make his journey to speaking a difficult one, however; Wesley had great difficulty with motor planning, so much so that typing out a sentence on his new app could take several minutes. It could be painful for his communication partners as they waited for his sentence to appear, reminding themselves not to interrupt or second-guess the rest of the sentence. Wesley was able to use this effectively, albeit slowly, to demonstrate that he had other hidden skills, such as the ability to read complex text in books and show good comprehension too. You could ask him a question about some novel text, and he would type out the correct answer every time. Wesley started to access oral motor exercises and tools linked directly to speech sounds and was soon able to start using a small number of consonant and vowel sounds. However, he found the effort required to move from one sound to another incredibly difficult. So although he appeared, on the one hand, motivated to gain verbal skills, he was easily disheartened with his very slow progress. No amount of reassurance that this was typical for a young person with verbal dyspraxia and his level of motor planning difficulty was enough; after several weeks he decided to take a break from therapy. Wesley's story at that time gave us an incredible insight into the potential situation of many young autistic children who are at the preverbal stage of communication. Perhaps they could make progress with speech, but perhaps it would also be very effortful and take a great deal of perseverance over a long time to achieve the level of speech that would gain them functional verbal communication skills. As much as we might be there cheering them on from the sidelines, giving them every encouragement to make their journey towards speech, we are not the ones feeling the frustrations and disappointments with every failed attempt at sound production or misproduction of a CV blend first hand. So it is understandable that for some young people, they decide that it is a mountain too high and too steep to climb. Then it is our job to help them to use the best AAC options for them to continue communicating their thoughts, ideas and opinions in alternative ways.

What we have found in many cases is that there are a group of children out there who will often have such a long period of focus on their receptive language skills, which are impacted so much by factors such as sensory needs and auditory memory limitations; as a result, they appear to make very poor progress and never get to the point where expressive communication is a focus for therapy. However, when we acknowledge their wider learning needs – for example, the sensory needs and any structural supports to help them understand tasks – we can be surprised at the underlying skills these children then show us. They are often much more motivated to take part and engage in therapy where expression is the goal, as it is something that allows them to share their wants, needs, thoughts, ideas and experiences, as well as to get tangible rewards for their efforts. Sometimes we get to see this transformation by taking a gamble and adding in our total speech approach with the expectation that speech is possible, even at times with no prior evidence that this is the case. The reward when you hear a child speak against all the odds is so much more special. Often as clinicians we come with our background of training and knowledge in all areas of communication, and we want to be recommending goals from gaps we identify during assessment. We are aware of the building blocks of typical early communication, and want to acknowledge the importance of all of these skills. However, when we listen to the concerns, the hopes and the dreams of parents who have a child who is still preverbal with complex needs, quite often what they really want is for their child to be given the opportunity to use their voice, to speak. They are their child's biggest cheerleader and will not often be happy with goals that cover many communication areas but not speech. After all, if a child is not following the typical developmental pattern so far, why should we still be following this in our advice and recommendations? Why not flip the communication pyramid on its head and aim straight for speech? This is exactly what we did with Florence. Florence was a very active little girl who loved to run and climb and hum. She was not keen on listening to instructions or conforming with group activities. She was also not particularly keen on looking at adults using signs and gesture, probably because this involved stopping for long enough to look at them and pay attention to what they were doing. We noticed that Florence paid attention most to music, and she would hum along to her favourite tunes. So we decided to sing along with her and offer her input for her sensory needs for touch and movement. For example, as she hummed 'head, shoulders, knees and toes', we would touch the different parts of her body, with our hands, or using textured beanbags – sometimes soft, sometimes bumpy or with a rough feel. If she was more active, we might stand in front of her on the trampette or on the swing, singing as she jumped and hummed along. She seemed to really respond positively to touch, with different textures on her arms and legs, as well as on her face. As we added touch to her face, she stilled long enough to look and use eye contact, smiled and shared different facial expressions. We used those moments to sing about what we were doing, sticking to Florence's favourite tunes. We then started adding in pictures to reinforce the words we were using. For example, pictures for 'head', 'shoulders', 'knees' and 'toes'. Florence began to study the pictures. Finally, we used tools to add sensory input to her mouth to prompt different speech sounds. At first Florence would just stop humming as a tool touched her mouth, but over time, she started to show more awareness of the parts of her face we were touching, and she began to respond with muscle movements too. Adding input to her lips, we started to see her consistently open, then close her lips. With the adult modelling the sound /b/ and showing her a picture to reinforce the same sound, everyone was delighted when one day Florence also said /b/. There then followed a string of babble, with the sound /b/ repeated over and over.

So what we are doing when we first meet these children and young people is meeting them at the point where they are at the time. If we find difficulties with listening to sounds, then we provide opportunities for them to develop these skills, through activities that help them to tune in and identify sounds at first within the environment, and then move onto sounds for speech. If we find difficulties with processing and storing sounds – in other words, with phonology – then we also work to help them develop their phonological awareness skills. Phonological awareness covers everything from word initial identification, to counting the number of syllables within a word, to rhyming skills. If a child has motor planning difficulties, then we support this by looking both at wider motor planning skills as well as a program to support this for speech. Finally, we look at the physical structures of the mouth to see if there's anything that might also be impacting on speech development. We consider related skills and needs, including response to different sensory information, preferred learning styles, literacy skills and motivation to access therapy. In short, we adopt a total speech approach. We will now focus on illustrating this eclectic approach to therapy, in the form of practical techniques and ideas for adapting within the classroom or home environment, during small group therapy as well as individual therapy sessions. As we do this, we will also be mapping therapy onto goals or targets, as we know these are also an integral part of both educational and health service requirements. You might choose to begin with the target, then use our ideas for ways to help achieve the target; or you might look for activities and techniques that are beginning to work for the child and use this to help you work out some appropriate targets.

6 | IEP/EHCP Target Bank

One of the things we have noticed over our years as therapists is when it comes to target setting for schools, there is often a gap in the area of speech clarity. Language and communication are covered in detail. Sometimes we differ in the order of goals, or we might debate the usefulness of some activities, but generally, the curriculum and target banks that go alongside have something to offer teachers. This means that language and communication targets often can be quite easily embedded into different lessons, and children work towards achieving their targets throughout the week. However, speech clarity is not something that most teachers would expect to find within the school's curriculum, beyond teaching for the 'speaking and listening' component and phonics. This is very much still the domain of the speech and language therapist/pathologist. So what we aim to do in this chapter is offer a range of functional targets that can be used for children with a range of speech needs. With each target, we suggest which techniques might be blended together to encourage progress, as well as ideas for practical games and activities to suit different ages or levels.

There is a useful strategy for building up to using the sounds for children who need longer to learn the sounds or to build up confidence for production. The strategy is 'match, select, name'. This means that you can begin by playing lots of games where the children just have to match the sound they hear with either the object or a picture. This helps to build up associations and vocabulary storage. When the children are confident at matching the sounds, then you can move on to 'select', where you play or say a sound and they have a selection of objects or pictures in front of them. Their task is to 'select' the correct object or picture. Finally, when they are confident at selecting, build up the expectation for them to say the sound or word themselves.

DOI: 10.4324/9781003340317-6

Targets That Focus on Experimenting With Vocal Sounds in Play

The following targets are for working on sounds within play, using environmental and onomatopoeic sounds, when children are able to make sounds but are often only using open vowels. These sounds help children to make early links between a sound sequence and a word meaning. To help with the physical production of the different sounds, you can try using the following techniques – use of video clips showing a close-up of your mouth making the sound for them to watch and copy; practise making the sounds in front of a mirror; using a 'big mouth' or puppet to get the mouth movements; if the sounds have clear consonants, try adding in some Cued Articulation for those sounds; for example, 'baaaa' would have the cued sign for /b/ at the beginning.

Target Set A – Achieving Transport Sounds

Ideas for games – have a big road mat on the floor, then have a bag of different vehicles. Take one out at a time, model the sound it makes, then pass it round the group for each child to have a turn. For this target, you could use video modelling so that the children can see your face as you model the sounds. Try to find a noisy book with buttons to press and hear different transport sounds. If the group is able to participate, create a scene that requires emergency vehicles to attend so that you can practise the sirens of the police car, fire engine and ambulance.

Target Set B – Achieving Animal Sounds

Ideas for games – pass around animal puppets, and when a child has a puppet, they have a go at making that animal's sound. Video modelling and use of Cued Articulation for any consonant sounds are recommended. Have a bag or a box filled with toy animals, and take turns to pick an animal and make the sound. This could also work with puppets of face masks. You can sing the song 'Old MacDonald Had a Farm' and the children can choose which animal, then they all join in with the animal sounds. Animal sound books with sound buttons and form board puzzles are also good for this target. Download a simple animal sounds app and play the sound, and see if the child can copy. This can be as silly as you like.

Target Set C – Achieving Environmental Sounds

Ideas for games – sing 'The Wheels on the Bus' to practise the sounds for the different bus parts. Have a toy house and a bag of toy house items such as a washing machine, telephone, a microwave, a doorbell, etc. Create role play where a character (led by the adult) is at home and goes around the group using the different items. As the character gets to each child, in turn they attempt to make the sound of their item and join in the play.

Download a simple transport sounds app and see if the child can copy.

For targets A, B and C earlier, what would really help is to see the suggested activities as just one component of 'therapy' or just one way to help teach these early skills. You would do well to start by helping the children to experience these sounds first hand. For example, if you are working on transport sounds, visit a transport museum, listen to the cars and buses as they go past your school, take a walk to the local railway station or airport. That way, when you play audio clips of transport, the children have memories to access, sounds that are stored more securely for them to then access and ultimately use. Similarly, for animal sounds, you would visit a farm or a zoo, listen to pets or visit a pet shop. Environmental sounds can be easier to access, such as a telephone ringing, the sound of the printer or school bell. At home, there will be opportunities for the children to listen to different sounds which you can then use in your sessions as follow-up. Depending on age and stage of the children in your class, why not set up an area for free play that also provides opportunities to listen and practise the target sounds? Toys in a tuff tray, transport or animal sound books on display or BIGMack buttons stuck on the wall for the students to press and hear the recorded sounds.

Targets That Focus on Achieving Specific Placements for Speech Sounds

The following targets are for working towards specific sounds when children are unable to copy them during phonics activities. We have included a range of activities all designed to support speech production. You can trial different activities until you have a selection that the child responds to well. It is not necessary to use all of the activities within each target set, so feel free to opt for your favourites, and omit those that do not work for you, the child or your setting.

Target Set A – Achieving the Bilabial Lip Sounds – m, p, b

Ideas for games – blow bubbles, catching them on the wand and popping on each child's lips. Use ice lolly sticks – place horizontally between your lips, and try to hold the stick in place. Add different sensations to the lips, for example, ice, yoghurt, custard, and encourage lip smacking. You could also use an electric toothbrush to add vibration to the lips for heightened sensory input. Follow all activities with attempts at the target sounds in order to link the oral motor activity with speech, even if this, at first, is mostly the adult producing the sounds for the children to hear. Model the use of Cued Articulation signs for these sounds to add more visual information about how the sounds are produced.

Target Set B – Achieving the Rounded Lip Sounds – oo, w, oh

Ideas for games – use straws, bubbles and party horns with round mouthpieces. Play games with the straws, such as blow football or painting. You can also use the straws to help blow bubbles! Try to play the party horns, and encourage the children to feel the shape of their lips. Why not show them in a mirror? After this sensory input, have a go at making the sound 'oo' – you could pretend to be monkeys, 'oo oo oo!' Then model and practise more rounded lip sounds including 'w' and 'oh'.

Target Set C – Achieving the Labiodental Sounds – f, v

Ideas for games – these sounds are still nice and visual, so using a mirror can help. Place food items onto the middle of the bottom lip that can then be scraped off with the top teeth. Make it into a game where the children have to sit on their hands or put their hands behind their backs – no cheating! The aim is to curl the bottom lip back until it meets the top teeth. Encourage the children to 'feel' where their teeth have just been before you ask them to try to repeat without the food. Ideas for bringing the sounds into activities include using a fishing rod and fish for pictures. You can have pictures of words beginning with /f/, such as fish, fox, fork, farm, food, face, fan and finger. You can use a toy van and push it noisily with a 'vvvvvvvrrooom' sound. The sound /v/ is fun to practise saying for a long time as you can feel it tickling the bottom lip – see if the children can feel it too!

Target Set D – Achieving the Elevated Tongue (Alveolar) Sounds – n, t, d, l

Ideas for games – you can use a mirror and also the food items from the 'f' and 'v' activities, but the placement will be different. Place the food just behind the top teeth, where the goal is for them to touch it with their tongue tips. After achieving the correct placement – this can take several attempts before they succeed, so do promote fun and encouragement in the process along the way – add in some of the target sounds. You might then play a game with 'teddy', and blow bubbles to touch his 'nose' and his 'lips' to model the sounds in words.

Target Set E – Achieving the Back Tongue (Velar) Sounds – k, g

Ideas for games – by now you will see a theme . . . yes, it's mirror and food items time! This time, place the item behind the middle bottom teeth for your tongue tip to find. At the same time, the back of the tongue raises up to touch the velum. This is really difficult for lots of children to do, and it is hard for them to 'see' when we model it in front of them. Try adding a mouth puppet with a tongue. First of all, show the group how to get the tongue into the right position, then see if they can help the puppet too! Finally, add in some words, and have some fun by playing 'ready, steady . . . Go! Racing cars down a track or a chute. Why not use castanets to make the clicking sound /k k k k k/ in a similar way to the Jolly Phonics action?

Targets That Focus on Achieving Different Communicative Functions

The following targets are for helping children to produce and then use simple core words with a very clear focus on word meaning, even when they may have a very restricted or limited verbal repertoire. Again, as Total Speech is not a prescriptive way of working, we encourage you to experiment with the activity ideas and put together a bank of activities that are best suited to the children you are supporting

Target – Achieving the Core Word 'More'

Ideas for games – use the tools for achieving /m/ from Set A above, then model how the mouth opens into a rounded shape with the long vowel sound. To model and rehearse the word, you can use anything that is quick-lasting, then you can create the opportunity for the children to ask for 'more'. Add in the sign for the word as you model the word. This works well with motivating foods, but you can also use different activities such as blowing bubbles, then pausing, or playing some music then stopping. Each time you pause or stop, you are waiting for the group to say 'more'.

Target – Achieving the Core Word 'Go'

Ideas for games – use the tools for achieving /g/ for Set E above, then getting activities, and this time you wait right at the beginning of the activity until the group tells you to 'go'. Games like a marble run, a car run and a ball run all work well. You can lead the session from the front if the group is able to maintain their attention, then the children can take turns to lead and let the thing 'go'. You can also add in races with cars or wind-up toys.

Target – Achieving the Core Word 'Stop'

Ideas for games – play 'dance and freeze', but say 'stop' instead. The 'st' at the beginning can be quite difficult, so you might hear 'top' or 'sop' – if this is the case, take the 's' and 'top' apart and repeat as separate parts for 5 times in a row before you attempt to blend them back together again. You could make a sound jigsaw by placing the 's' and 'top' together. Add the 'Cued Articulation sign for the /s/ sound as a reminder.

Target – Achieving the Core Word 'No'

Ideas for games – play games where you find out things the group members really like, then add in something at the end that they have a firm dislike for. For example, 'Do you like chocolate?' (yes) 'Do you like raisins?' (yes) 'Do you like breadsticks?' (yes) 'Do you like sprouts? 'No!' Perhaps there are certain songs that people dislike, or maybe they don't like to be tickled, or they dislike bubbles being popped on their face. Once you know the group's dislikes, you have the opportunities to rehearse saying 'no'. Use the sign for 'no', and show the 'no' symbol to reinforce meaning.

Target – Achieving the Core Word 'Help'

Ideas for games – screw the lid on tubs or bottles of motivating items and pass them round the group, inviting the children to ask for 'help' to open them up. Give a child a packet of crisps or unopened wrapped biscuit/yogurt. Often children will struggle to blow up a balloon, so you can give everyone a balloon, then when they struggle, they need 'help', and you can blow one up for them to keep or let fly around the room. Giving any item that requires that 'adult input' (a spinning top?) and putting your hand on something, for example, a door handle, also presents an opportunity to ask for help.

Target – Achieving the Core Word 'Want' (or 'Need')

'I want to go!' 'I want more!' 'What do you want?' 'I want that!' The word 'want' can be used in any setting and is one of the most frequently used words by preschoolers.

The word 'want/need' is often used to request something with an increased sense of urgency. Many children (and adults) tend to exaggerate the urgency of a desire by using this word (e.g. 'I need candy' or 'I need pizza').

We can teach the meaning of the word 'want' without depriving our students of their basic needs. Try gently sabotaging the environment by giving your child yoghurt with no spoon to elicit 'I want a spoon', or putting them in the bathtub with no water to elicit 'I want water.'

The word 'want' can be used to comment on items that are missing or lacking. Ideas for games: try teaching this concept when playing with toys like Mr. Potato Head or dolls. Model phrases like 'he wants a nose' or 'she wants a dress'.

Target – Achieving the Core Word 'Hello'/'Bye' (Greetings)

The aim here is for the child to achieve some kind of a greeting, which is naturally a very social function. This can be achieved by saying 'hi/hello/ hiya/bye/see ya' at the points in experience in which these words occur. Joining in songs/rhymes or joining in peekaboo activities at these points too can also present an opportunity to use these words. Often at the start of activities, a 'hello' song would be used, and similarly, at the end of the activity, when it's time to finish, to say goodbye. Sometimes the child may already be using a gesture (wave) at this point, but speech may be absent, so it is a meaningful way to develop and link together the non-verbal communication with the speech.

Target – Achieving a Request for an Action (Child Asks an Adult to Perform an Action (Verbs)

The focus here is often for the child to be able to *make* an adult do something.

Such as 'push me' on a swing or 'carry me' or 'blow' for bubbles or 'eat' for a snack. Verbs are not only a powerful way to get a child to communicate but they are flexible too and can be used as a pivot words with lots of other words. They lead easily into two-word combinations. Techniques for encouraging this lie in everyday routines and activities, such as time at the local park, or fun actions that are motivating for the child to see, like 'spray' with a spray bottle so that someone else gets wet, or 'tickle' so that the adult tickles a peer.

Target – Achieving the Question Words 'Who?' 'Where?' 'What?' 'When?' 'Why?'

The ability to ask questions is something that is key to having conversations with others, either to initiate or to maintain conversation, and it can be difficult to find ways of teaching this as a skill to children who are not yet asking questions. The key to this target is creating curiosity to the extent that the children are desperate to find out the answers! 'Who?' might be achieved by using a 'reveal' picture to eventually reveal the faces of people who are familiar, such as peers, teachers, family members of popular characters relating to the group's interests. To encourage use of 'where?' you can play a game of hide-and-seek, or hide something around the room for the children to look for, especially something very motivating that can be rewarding when they find it. For 'what?' a popular activity is to have a bag or box that is full of interesting and exciting toys, and the children have to guess 'what' is in the bag or box. The activity is usually introduced using a song, and anticipation is built by shaking or tapping on the bag or box before revealing the items one by one. Questions are really good for rehearsing the sounds /h/ and /w/, so using bubble blowing is a great way to warm up and create the initial sounds for the question words. If you catch a bubble on the bubble wand, you can then take turns to breathe out with a long /h:/ sound to wobble the bubble before blending into the word 'who'. When lip rounding is gained, blow bubbles through the bubble wand, then recreate the lip rounding shape to move onto /w/ for 'what' and 'where'.

Targets That Focus on Different Word Structures

Whether a child has a speech delay, a consistent phonological disorder, an inconsistent phonological disorder or verbal dyspraxia, you may notice that certain word structures are affected more than others. With motor planning difficulties associated with verbal dyspraxia, you will typically want to work through the following structures in order; however, other children may be able to focus straight away on a particular structure that is more complex. This structure is represented in the Nuffield Dyspraxia Programme.

- Single sound production.
- Single sound alternations.
- Consonant-Vowel (CV) blends/Vowel-Consonant (VC) blends.
- CVCV words.
- CVC words.

So if the target sounds are the early bilabial (lip) sounds, you might come up with the following list of sounds and words to work through:

- m – m – m – m – m   p – p – p – p – p   b – b – b – b – b.

Say the sounds as you tap, hit, pop, shake or jump. Say the sounds as you visually move along a counter, or add dots with a pen.

- m – p – m – p – m   p – b – p – b – p   m – b – m – b – m.

Show the difference between the sounds by holding up sound cards as you alternate, or use the Cued Articulation signs. You can also use the Talk Tools™ apraxia shapes to help them see and feel the difference if needed.

- more, moo, my, may, me pea, poo, pay, pie, paw baa, bee, boo, bow, bye.

Take each word and aim for multiple repetitions during a group session before adding in more words. When words are accurate by themselves, try alternating between two distinctly different words to combine into a phrase, for example, 'more pie', 'my bow', 'bye bee'. Listen out for the vowel sounds too, taking care to model them back accurately if you have any children who struggle to distinguish between different vowels when speaking.

- arm, am, um, I'm up, ape orb.

You can stretch out the sounds to help with blending if the children find it hard to copy the whole word straight away, for example, 'aarmmmm' for 'arm'. Some children may also find it easier at first to leave a short gap in between the 2 sounds, although some practitioners advise against this. In our experience, it really is different for every child, so try at first to encourage them to copy the full CV/VC word, but then consider breaking the sounds apart if needed.

- Mummy, money, marble, summer, hammer puppy, people, party, happy, pony bubble, bunny, baby.

This is the first stage where you have more than one syllable, so you can help the group to 'notice' this by clapping both the syllables as you say them. You could mark the syllables in lots of different ways, such as stomping feet, playing a drum or using 'robot arms'. Words that have the same consonant sound for both syllables will be easier than words that have 2 different sounds, so 'mummy' would usually be easier than 'money'.

- map bam bap boom beep mop beam.

When children first attempt the CVC level, they can find it particularly difficult. Something you may notice includes omitting the final sound, so 'map' becomes 'ma', and 'boom' becomes 'boo'; this is known as 'final consonant deletion', or FCD for short. If you do notice this, help the child to hear the final sound by repeating back and emphasising the final sound. Try writing the word down or using magnetic letters, and highlight the final sound visually. You can also help them to add the final sound by using Cued Articulation or apraxia shapes for the final sound production. Another thing that may occur at this stage is the child adds an extra vowel sound on the end of the word. This happens because they are so far used to words with either CV or CVCV structure, and it is something that many children do at first. Try not to focus too much, just model back the correct version, and you will often find that the extra vowel sound soon disappears. If you do want to try to eliminate this sound, aim to increase awareness of the word structure; for example, it only has one syllable – clap once as you say the word and talk about any sounds that you can hear after the clap and how they don't belong to the word; or show the word visually, and look to see which sound is the last sound in the word to be produced. See if the child can hear the difference in both yours and their own productions.

Following these stages, you can continue to add challenge by looking at words with consonant blends, for example, 'spoon' or 'blue', and words that have 3 or more syllables – also referred to as 'multisyllabic words', such as 'bu - tter - fly' and 'ca - ter - pi - llar'. Often, by the time you reach these later stages, you will notice that many of the children will have continued to improve in speech clarity without the need to continue having a special focus, so your group numbers may shrink, or you may need to group children differently according to their new needs. It is also worth thinking about how to support children with generalisation of new speech skills into the classroom and beyond. For example, do you have visual prompts in different classroom areas, or perhaps stuck to their desk? Bookmarks illustrated with the target sounds can be another really useful way to reinforce and embed practise in reading and during story times. For ideas to work on different sound placements, including alveolar, velar and labiodental placements, see Table A.1 in the appendix.

Not all children move from clear single words all the way to clear speech in conversation without further direct input, even if you are able to support generalisation across the day in lots of different activities. This is where you can continue to use the later sections of the Nuffield Dyspraxia Programme. Initially, combine 2 words together using a 'pivot' word such as 'no' which you can add to your target words. For example, if you have managed to achieve clarity for CVC words on their own, you might then have phrases such as 'no cake', 'more cake', 'no cat' 'no bike', 'no fish'. After 2-word combinations, move onto 3-word combinations, then longer phrases and finally full sentences. The published Nuffield programme has its own phrases and sentences, but it is nice to create bespoke phrases and sentences that are more meaningful to the children you are supporting. You can have the current list of phrases and sentences typed out and rehearsed at set times during the day. The more frequently they are practised, the quicker they will become clear and embedded in everyday speech. If a child already uses a visual timetable or planner, why not add 'speech practice' to their timetable? This will help to encourage independence and ownership for their speech work, which is good to promote.

7 | Running a Total Speech Group

Much of our clinical experience has been working within specialist schools, where the children have often had speech needs as part of their overall profile of needs. Whereas we would often support the inclusion of language and communication goals throughout the day in various lessons, speech goals have often been more specific to the individual child and can be harder to embed without additional adult time and support. So alongside 1 to 1 support for those children whose specific speech needs have indicated this, we have often looked at running intervention for small groups. Sometimes this has worked within a class, where we would run the speech group for half of the class (small class size) while the other half would access another school area, then swap the groups so that we would work with all of the class over 2 sessions. Where there has not been a general need in class for this input, we have run groups where children have joined each other from different classes and come together for speech as a specific intervention. Either way, the group atmosphere has lent itself well to meeting many different needs. It has been a great way to reinforce access to group activities and following group rules; it has allowed children to see others completing exercises and activities as additional modelling and helped to reduce anxiety as well as deflect attention from themselves; it has also offered opportunities for shared enjoyment and social communication.

Getting started: before you begin running the group, you will need to know as much as possible about the students' abilities in different areas, including listening, phonics, reading, sound production, as well as any sensory-seeking or avoidance behaviours. Decide on the aims of the group; for example, do you have a core group of sounds you would like them to achieve? Do you want them to have improved

DOI: 10.4324/9781003340317-7

listening and identification of sounds? Perhaps your aim for some students is to build up tolerance and acceptance for sensory input? You should have overall goals for the group and then you will of course begin to differentiate according to individual needs on top of this.

Next, have a think about the different materials you will need. For example, are you going to use any songs, and if so, will you be singing them, playing them, listening to them or watching them on a screen? A song we have used before is the 'Parts of Face' song available on YouTube, but you might have an alternative you prefer. When exploring and using horns as part of our oral motor input, we might sing, 'I Am the Music Man' and encourage the children to play their horns along to the song. We would often have a range of tools for improving phonation and lip skills, including bubbles and horns. For detailed information about the horns and bubbles hierarchies, please refer to the Talk Tools Oral Placement Therapy programme (Rosenfeld-Johnson, 2009). A pot of bubbles with good bubble mixture can be used to pop a bubble onto the lips to feel and increase awareness of lip closure for the sounds /m/, /p/ and /b/. You can then catch a bubble on the wand and practise using oral airflow to breathe on the bubble with a long /h/ sound and watch the bubble wobble for extra visual feedback. Then we would see if the children can blow bubbles themselves. If they can, do they blow with spread lips, or can they round and protrude their lips as they blow? If they use spread lips, we would then use short tubes or straws to help them position their lips ready for blowing. This then moves onto the sounds /u:/ ('oo' as in 'boo') and /w/. When it comes to the horns, think about the shape of the mouthpiece. If you are wanting to focus on lip closure still, look for horns that have a flat mouthpiece; whereas horns with round mouthpieces will help to achieve lip rounding. Other tools for sensory input can include cloths or beanbags made from a different material that can be used in facial massage to increase awareness of different parts of the face, such as cheeks, chin and lips. This can make a good accompaniment to the 'Parts of the Face Song', with either an adult helping the child by massaging with the material, or the children using this themselves to add tactile input for awareness before using different parts of their faces, and mouths for sounds. We do tend to find that the tools used are often intrinsically motivating for the children, but for children who perhaps struggle more with the sensory input, consider whether or not to add in things that could be used as rewards or motivation to take part in the activities. Finally, to ensure that any speech work is linked to meaningful language, have a bag or box of items to model language in a functional way. For example, if you have focused on lip closure for /m/, /p/ and /b/, you might then have a bubble machine to model the words 'bubble', 'pop', and 'more'; you might have a baby doll and a ball that you can bounce to baby. Baby can then pat the ball, or perhaps baby hides so you can model the word 'boo!'.

How to Plan the Group Format

When our speech work includes a range of approaches, it makes sense to work in order from awareness activities through to production, then finish with functional games to apply any words covered in a meaningful way. Awareness activities can include things like talking or singing about the parts of the mouth, listening awareness to identify different speech sounds, as well as sensory awareness from input such as massage or touch location. So when they hear a sound, can they identify the sound by naming it, or pointing a picture representation of the sound? For children who are able to do so, you can discuss where in the mouth the sound is produced, for example, with both lips, the tongue tip, with a high or low jaw height, etc. Look to see whether children need support to increase their mouth awareness, or specific parts of the mouth. Can they feel where touch is applied when they are not looking? If you talk about different mouth parts, can they touch or point to the correct parts? Your responses to these questions will help you to plan awareness activities that will both cue your group in as well as help to improve their skills in this area. You might need to differentiate for different group members, and don't forget to have a way of documenting baseline skills and progress during group intervention sessions. For the production section, think carefully about the sounds you would like to target. Will it be the same set of sounds for the whole group? How long will you need to spend on each sound – will you be rotating the sounds, or does your group need a high level of repetition in order to learn new concepts, including speech sounds? When you have identified the sounds you would like to work on, think about how you can introduce and teach them. This might include thinking about whether the sound is easy to 'see' when you say it, for example, the sound /b/ is very visual as the lips come together when the sound is produced; whereas the sound /g/ is produced further back in the mouth, so it is harder to 'see' what is happening. Knowing about the way sounds are produced can help with imitation and with the 'feel' of a sound. For example, some sounds are 'plosives' with 2 places coming together with a firm contact. Plosives are also known as 'stops' because the movement stops in a particular place. Examples of this kind of sound are /p, b, t, d, k, g/. Some sounds are known as 'fricatives', which involve the air flowing between 2 points in the mouth, creating friction – hence the name 'fricative'. These sounds can also be referred to as 'hissing' sounds as they make a long sound, and you can hear the air flowing or escaping as the sound is produced. Examples are /f, s, z/.

At the end of a group, we recommend linking the group's target sounds to function and meaning. Choose a fun game or activity that allows you to model the sounds in words and sentences. For example, if your target sounds were /m, p, b/ to work on lip closure, you might then use a bubble machine to incorporate the words 'more' 'pop' and 'bubbles'; or perhaps you could offer snacks and model the words 'more' 'popcorn' and 'biscuit'. If you have been focusing on sounds at the back of the mouth such as /k/ and /g/, you might play with 'cars' and model 'go' as you push them down a track. In these activities, if you have group members who have not yet been successful with production, use it as an opportunity for modelling and listening without any pressure to join in with speech; however, for children who are doing well at producing the sounds in isolation, you can encourage them to have turns at saying the words during the activity. Saying words together can be easier than them speaking by themselves at first. You can then fade out your support when they get more confident.

When you have set up the group to match the needs of your group members, you should find that they participate willingly, and it is often a lot of fun. However, for some children with more complex needs, especially if their needs include an element of sensory aversion, this may mean more careful planning to ensure they get the most out of the group. Some things to consider – identifying individual goals that the children are aware of, then including a reward structure so that they are motivated to try. Some children will need instant rewards throughout the group; however, others may be able to wait until the group has finished before receiving their reward. Another way to manage varying levels of need within one group can be the use of a 'layered group'. This works by including all the children right at the start, but each time an activity ends, there is an opportunity for one or some of the children to peel away from the group to access child-led play or a sensory break. This allows for all the children to attend fully for as long as they are able. The reverse can also work well, in which some children join in just at the end of the group and gradually work up to participating in more of the activities earlier on.

As well as planning the structure of the group with all the relevant activities to meet the group members' needs, decide on the size of the group and how many supporting adults you may need. This is particularly key when it comes to any Talk Tools exercises if the children need support and supervision to be able to use them correctly, or to keep them as therapy tools, not toys. We have delivered Total Speech groups of many different sizes, from 2:2 ratio up to 2:8. Where possible, try to keep each child's tools separate so they can be easily accessed and updated, as well as personalised to match and progress with oral motor skills. Here are three groups that we have run to give you an idea of how they might look, and to illustrate just how varied they can be!

Group 1 – Developing Skills Through Experience and Motivation

One of the first times Karen ran a Total Speech group, it was planned jointly with the class teacher in a specialist primary school where I had been working for 2 years. There were 6 pupils in the class, each with a significant level of learning disability as well as a diagnosis of autism. In order to gain the most from the group time, we decided that as well as the adult leading the group, each group member would be fully supported 1 to 1. We ran two groups back to back, so that meant 4 adults and 3 pupils in each group. The groups lasted approximately 15 minutes each. Before the pupils entered the room, sensory calming music was played on a whiteboard with calming visual patterns. The pupils entered quietly one by one and sat next to their supporting adult, with their pack of tools under their chairs. We brought in some visual communication aids that were familiar from the classroom, so after a minute of calm, a yellow traffic light circle was shown to all the group members to indicate 'one more minute' before the first activity. The red traffic light circle signalled the end of the music, which was then muted, and a green traffic light shown to indicate the first activity – 'facial massage has started'. At this cue, the adults took the pupils' facial massagers from their packs. This could be as simple as an electric toothbrush, or a tool with different shaped or textured ends. For any pupils who needed more support to tolerate vibration, or they were hypersensitive to touch, they would use a normal toothbrush or a pair of soft beanbags for more subtle sensory input. We then moved onto chewing activities to move the jaw, and we would link this to different vowel sounds during Intensive Interaction as well as offering a snack. To help with other areas of need such as flexibility with foods, we introduced different crunchy and chewy foods. Communication skills were brought in by offering choices and providing symbols to aid specific requests. We then used bubbles and horns to help them develop their phonation skills, as well as coordinating breathing with lip closure, linked then to the sounds /m, p, b/ again through Intensive Interaction. Finally, we would end with 2 more minutes of sensory calming music. Over the course of a year, there were many gains, including improved oral motor skills, wider range of sounds used, greater flexibility with food and improved focus for social interaction. In addition to these gains, supporting staff reported that the sessions were very relaxing and enjoyable, and the pupils attended willingly. Some children relaxed more during the group than at other times and made progress with group participation as they enjoyed the activities.

Group 2 – Developing Skills to Support Early Speech and Literacy

The next group of children formed half of a nursery class – ages 3 and 4 – also in a special school. Their needs were different to the group described above. Again, there were 5 children attending the group, but the ratio was slightly different, with 4 adults in total, including the group leader. Not all children were still preverbal, both those who did have some speech were still unintelligible or had few spoken words. Most had delayed eating and drinking skills, such as not yet able to drink from an open cup or a straw, or unable to chew different textured foods. The group ran within the nursery room and began again with music, but this time it was a song called 'Parts of the Face Song', encouraging the children to learn the words for different parts of their face. The parts of the face were labelled, which also encouraged the children's reading skills. As different parts were mentioned in the song, adults would support the children to identify and touch the relevant parts, using facial massage for those children who could tolerate this. After building awareness, both cognitively, linguistically and physically, we moved onto the jaw for chewing skills and grading needed for smooth transition between sounds and placements. Each child began with a chewy tube and was supported to chew on both sides of their mouth. The supporting adult checked if they were able to chew up and down, if they compressed the tube completely or just nibbled. They also looked out for any jaw sliding from side to side – at which point more support was given or the tube was discontinued. We then introduced the bubble blowing activity, popping bubbles on the lips for lip closure and the sounds /m, p, b/, then blowing bubbles for rounded lips and the sounds 'oo' and 'w'. If a child needed support with this, they had a short tube or straw to blow through, supporting their lips in the correct shape. Next we used horns to practice coordinating lip placement with breath control. We used the song 'I am the Music Man' to encourage the children to play along. Finally, all the activities were presented on a 'choose board' so that children could request a repeat of their favourite activity at the end. We found that again, the children and adults enjoyed the group, and it led to discussions of how some activities could be supported and extended in other ways during the nursery day. For example, during sensory play activities, straws were added to blow bubbles around in the water tray, or to make patterns with paint in a tuff tray. During snack time, the children who needed more help with jaw work in group were offered strips of food that would encourage chewing; if they had struggled with rounded lips for blowing bubbles or horns, they would be supported to drink through a straw; if they had difficulty with lip closure, then they would drink from an open cup.

Group 3 – Developing Specific Speech Sounds in a Multi-sensory Way

This group was run as a whole class, who were all developing their speech and literacy skills. They had a range of needs, including learning difficulties, those associated with Down syndrome, and autism. This time, we had a particular sound focus that linked in with their phonics work in class, as well as being a sound some children found difficult to produce for speech. One term we focused on the sound /f/. To begin with, we sang a quick 'hello' to each other, and identified the focus sound by holding up a big 'f' sound picture. We used Cued Articulation to sign the sound as we attempted to say it. Then the class listened to a story all about a girl called 'Fiona' who went on a journey finding many different things that began with 'f'. We paused each time there was something new, to highlight the sound 'f', to label the word and look at the written letter. After the story, we used the 'f' words from the book in a fishing game. This way, the children took turns to fish for a word, turn it over and say it out loud. The fishing game allowed them to hear the target sound modelled repeatedly as each child was called up to 'fish' and 'find' a word. Finally, we would talk about how the sound was produced, using mirrors as the children tried to copy the action of curling back their bottom lips against their top teeth. If children needed extra sensory input to achieve the placement, we used small round cereal stuck to the bottom lip for them to try to bite off, allowing them to feel the scraping action of the teeth against the lip. Another time we focused on the sound 'c/k', so we followed a similar format but changed the activities. The book was called 'My "k" Book', and this time all the key words began with the sound /k/. We then used the words at the end of a car run. Each time the car reached the bottom of the run, it landed on the top picture, which was turned over, and the child who pushed the car would attempt the word. When it came to looking in the mirrors and talking about how to produce the sound, we used lolly sticks to hold down the front of the tongue and help the back raise up to produce the sound. There is also a Cued Articulation sign to reinforce the correct position for production. We would finish the group by recapping what we had done, including the focus sound, any words we had rehearsed, and then brainstormed ideas for caring on with the practice within different activities throughout the week. With both the children and teaching team present for this discussion, it helped to ensure the carry-over took place beyond the focused sessions.

Carry-over Ideas

Here are just some of the ways that you can support the carry-over practice of sounds within the classroom, particularly when different children have different focus sounds:

1) Each child creates a 'My Sound Book' with their number one focus sound on the front. The daily schedule or timetable includes 'My Sound Book' so that the children are prompted to go and take their books for sound work. This can then last for as little or as long as time will allow in class. Perhaps it could feature just before a 'free play' or 'choose' time so that each child works to their own attention span before moving on. For example, Molly might manage 10 minutes work before she needs to play, whereas Michael might only focus for 5 minutes before he gets tired and needs to finish. The sound books then get gradually filled with different text or pictures relating to that sound, and the child practises the words within their book each day.

2) Create sound bookmarks to act as reminders when it comes to reading time. The reminder is as helpful to the child as it is to the supporting adults – don't forget to send a bookmark home too so that generalisation can take place more consistently and at a faster rate. If a child has more than one or two target sounds, it might be helpful to make different bookmarks, each with a different sound reminder. Then use one bookmark (one sound focus) at a time until progress can be seen, before swapping for a different bookmark (a different sound).

3) Talk about the goals with the whole class. Often there will be other children in the class who will remember which children need to practise specific sounds – in the same way that when a group of people goes to restaurant to order food, some group members will always remember who ordered what food. This not only removes pressure from teaching staff to remember but also helps to foster independence and peer support within the classroom.

4) Thread goals through different curriculum subjects by focusing on words that can be repeated in different contexts, or by identifying a set of words for each lesson. For example, if the goal is to use /s/ blends in word initial position, you might choose to set up opportunities for them to say 'stop', you could create 'snap' picture games based on different topic vocabulary, you could play 'I spy', you could choose between the 'swing' or the 'slide' at the local park or allow a turn to 'spin' on a computer chair. If the goal was to use the sound /f/ in word initial, you could create opportunities to count items out from one to five in the different lessons, repeating 'four' and 'five' each time.

How Long and How Frequently?

We find that whenever we recommend any new type of intervention or technique, there are some questions that people naturally will ask. Some of the answers have been covered in our descriptions of the group format and preparation of above; however, what we have not covered is the length and frequency of the group sessions. Length really depends on the structure of your day and the attention span of the children in your group. There is no right or wrong, and we have seen children engage for everything from just 5 minutes up to a 30-minute session. In terms of frequency, the answer really is as simple as the more frequent you are able to run this kind of group, the quicker you are likely to see results. As a minimum, once per week would allow for a predictable routine, and you would then be able to plan in some carry-over activities at other times and perhaps also send ideas for homework activity too. Another option time allows is to have a daily group feature in place of another regular session, such as 'morning group' or registration, or perhaps finishing a late morning lesson earlier and setting aside 10 minutes prior to lunchtime. You should also consider whether or not this is something that you will run all through the academic year or whether you will run it for a half term or term before evaluating progress. This again will depend on the children in your group and how quickly you expect to see progress occurring. Children receiving individual speech sound therapy will often make gains if seen for 8–10 sessions, so a full term's intervention would be ideal in that case; however, if learning is a known difficulty, you might find that repetition over a full year is necessary.

8 | Total Speech – the Pathway

Since spending time working with so many children and young people and analysing how and when they made progress in different areas, we began to see patterns. This led to the creation of a visual aid to map out the route from preverbal to verbal, showing where different skills and approaches might be introduced in order to help children make progress. We cover the journey before speech as well as after speech, which, in some ways, mirrors the communication pyramid; however, the approaches mentioned are all used with the end goal of speech production, which means that we never lose sight of this goal as we move forwards. You will see that we also clearly mark with a dotted line the point where pre-intentional communication turns into intentional communication, and this can be a pivotal moment in terms of how we can support the speech process more directly. Bear in mind this is just a general guide. Of course, we know that some children will respond better to some approaches than others. Sometimes children make sudden leaps forwards unexpectedly and perhaps in spite of the work we are doing in other areas. None of our work is intended to be prescriptive, always descriptive and encouraging of an eclectic approach to speech therapy. Remember the individual child in front you is your starting point, and a bespoke formula is always the best way forwards. In this chapter we are going to talk through each of the techniques outlined in the map below.

Pre-intentional

At the pre-intentional stage is where we can really shift the way we think about speech production. On meeting children who appear to

DOI: 10.4324/9781003340317-8

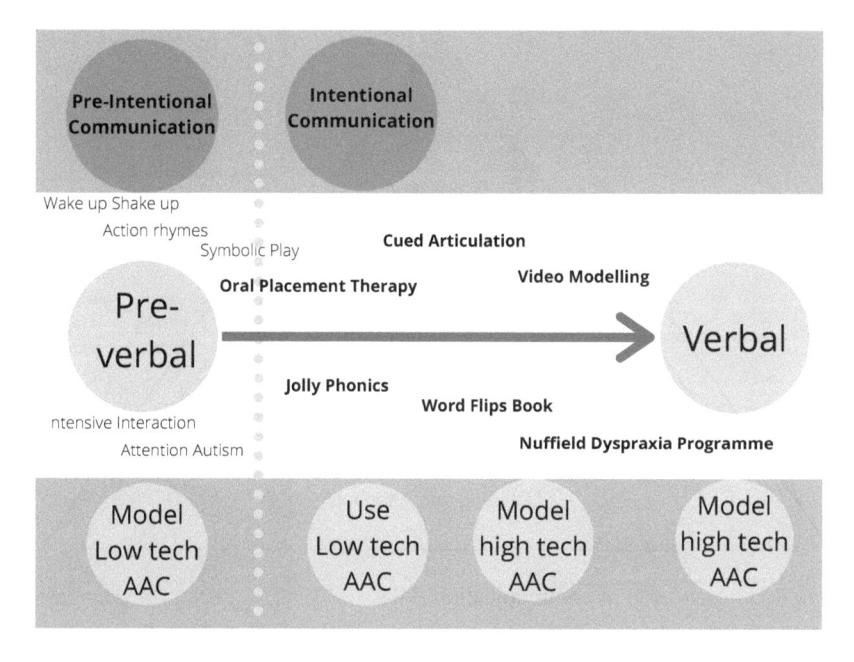

Figure 8.1 Key therapy approaches from preverbal to verbal communication

behave and move around 'in their own bubble', children who do not necessarily pay much attention to others and often do not respond to their own name, we might be drawn to the bottom of the communication pyramid. At the bottom we see the label 'Listening and Attention', so we begin by addressing only those skills directly linked to listening and attention.

The goals we set at this level can make a big difference to how everyone perceives our involvement, the level of expectation we are setting for the future and can also impact on our relationship with key family members at the outset of therapy. So how do we address this to ensure that we are helping to build those early building blocks of communication while at the same time working on speech sound goals? Well, we begin by setting our overall therapy goal as helping to transform the child from preverbal to verbal. We aim to move from pre-intentional to intentional, so that we end up with a child who is intentionally speaking to communicate with others. For example, rather than setting a goal for a child to listen and pay attention during a small group activity, we could set goals for child to listen

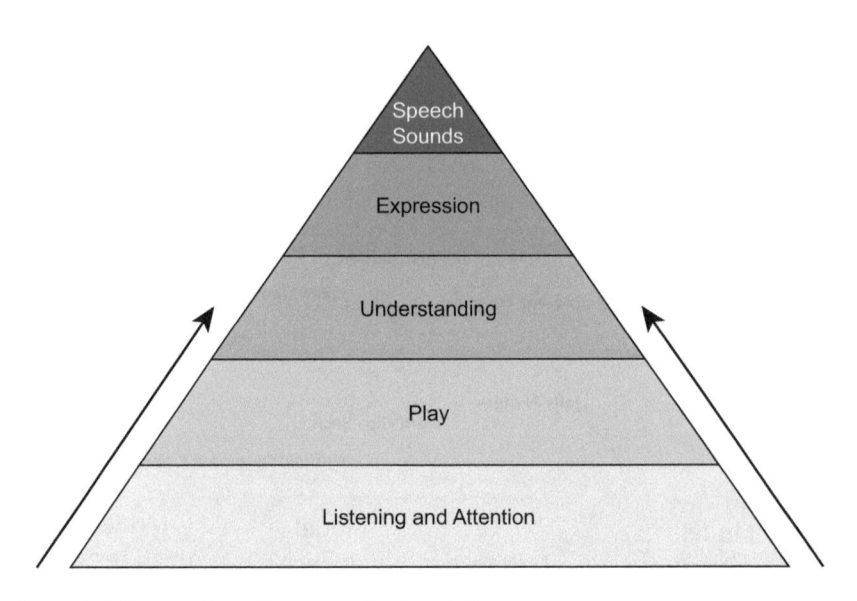

Figure 8.2 Progression of communication skills

and pay attention to sounds in order to begin tuning in to speech. What we do and how we do it would likely stay the same, but our focus might be slightly different; and by mentioning the word 'speech', we would automatically assume that we are working towards this verbal outcome rather than somewhere much lower down the triangle or pyramid. On the subject of expectations, we have had many conversations with other people – including parents but also teaching professionals, speech and language professionals, paediatricians and psychologists – who have indicated that a child may never learn to talk, or that they would be happy if they could just indicate their basic wants and needs somehow (not necessarily verbally). In making these statements, the expectations automatically lower, and the team around the child become quite pessimistic when looking ahead to the child's communication potential – which of course is only ever a guessing game, as we do not really know how a child will go on to develop into the future no matter how many clues we may currently have at our disposal.

If we expect more speech from someone, we will automatically begin to create more opportunities for speech to occur, which will in turn lead to the likelihood of that child speaking being much higher. Even though we value different forms of communication, and we do also support children to access and use alternative communication, we know that there have been studies that show how people respond more to children who are verbal compared to those who are not. There are two more reasons why we feel it is important to work towards speech. The first reason is that 'speech' is nearly always what parents have as their first goal, so if we can share their goal, then we automatically start off on the same track. The second reason is that, although we can recommend and trial different methods of communication such as signs and symbols, not all children are happy to use these alternative methods and will hold out for their own voices to develop in order to send their messages to others. Therefore, when we are working with them on their speech, they become much more motivated to engage in therapy and have more success as a result of this motivation and cooperation with therapy and 'homework' practice.

Wake Up Shake Up and Action Rhymes

Returning to the graphic above, we have identified 'wake up shake up' and 'action rhymes' as useful activities to begin thinking about speech as a goal during the pre-intentional communication stage. If you are not familiar with 'wake up shake up', it is something often seen in schools either as a large group in the school hall or perhaps a class of children gathering together. At the front of the group, an adult will lead with actions to music, designed to 'wake up' and 'shake up' the body, as a sensory alerting activity. Both movement and music are ways of reaching children with all levels of ability as language and cognitive skills are not needed in order to access this activity. Before a child is able to imitate the actions, they can be supported to do so, hand over hand. This helps to create muscle memory and motor patterns to access when imitation skills are ready. Action rhymes, where songs are accompanied by different hand actions, are also good to encourage, with support to help children make the actions if they do not readily copy. At first sight, these activities may not seem obviously linked to speech; however, if we view speech as a fine motor activity, we can then see how there is an incremental progression from gross motor movements and skills to fine motor movements and skills. This begins in infancy as babies develop strength, coordination and positional awareness through sitting, turning their heads and crawling. It ultimately leads to more sophisticated tasks such as writing, doing up buttons and zips and speaking. If we can help children to start imitating gross motor movements with their hands, this will then develop to more refined motor movements with signing and pointing, leading to imitation of mouth movements and then speech sounds. There is a useful article from the Hanen Centre explaining in more detail how imitation links to social interaction and language production, including tips for helping imitation skills in autistic children.

Therefore, working on imitation is going to be key to supporting a child from left to right along our speech graphic, through early social skills to language to speech.

Intensive Interaction

Intensive Interaction was developed as a widely recognised approach by Dave Hewett and Melanie Nind when they met in the 1980s. It moved things away from adult-led task-oriented approaches to working with children and adults at the pre-intentional, preverbal stage of communication. The approach is based on the interaction between infant and caregiver during the first 12 months of life, which is led by the child. The caregiver joins the infant in his sounds and actions and makes gradual adjustments in volume, pace and intonation as the interactions develop over time and become more sophisticated. The initial connection centres around being comfortable in each other's company but goes on to include sharing physical contact, eye contact and facial expressions, sending messages back and forth as early 'conversations'. The involvement and responsive nature of the adult right from the beginning encourages and creates multiple opportunities for the child or learner to make progress in all the foundations for successful speech or verbal communication. Speech attempts are encouraged and rewarded. The powerful connection created is the perfect environment for tuning in and allowing for imitation so that the child can begin to copy the adult's new sounds that are a variation on their existing repertoire. In terms of the communication pyramid, this approach manages to support progress in all areas, right through from attention and listening to speech sounds and everything in between. If there is one approach you might want to add to your toolkit, then this is definitely that one approach. Intensive Interaction is still an important tool to use when a child has crossed over the dotted line and is speaking verbally, because they may still need help to build the earlier communication skills for social interactions; they may also continue to rely on adult modelling of new language and phrases for different situations. The technique is also one that is applicable regardless of any underlying medical or neurodevelopmental condition that may have contributed to a child's preverbal and pre-intentional communication level. In our clinical experiences, this has included children with a description of 'profound and multiple learning difficulties' and/or diagnosis of autism spectrum disorder (ASD).

Attention Autism

Attention Autism is an intervention model that was designed by Speech and Language Therapist Gina Davies in order to create visually enticing activities that encouraged the learner to come and pay attention, then stay to learn. The activities used within this approach should allow the children or learners to come over without needing to be coaxed or rewarded for doing so, in being naturally entertaining and inherently interesting. The approach is divided into 4 stages, where stage 1 is the earliest and easiest for children to access, and stage 4 requires more developed attention skills. Central to its purpose is helping children to focus not just on the object or item of interest but, first of all, on the adult who is leading the session. By placing the adult as the key point of interest, the children will naturally be more likely to pick up on social cues such as facial expression, eye contacts, mouth shapes and movements for speech. Stage 1 includes 'the bucket', with the lead adult building both attention and suspense by singing a short song, then taking off the lid to look inside. The adult then plays with the highly engaging objects taken from the bucket for 3–5 minutes as the children sit and watch. Then the bucket lid is replaced, followed by a high-interest, fun activity. Stage 2 expects attention to build as the bucket items are played with for a longer a period of time, and anticipation skills are honed. In stage 3, the session becomes interactive as children take turns to participate in the activity. They also begin to shift their attention as different people take turns. Finally, in stage 4, the group attend for adult-led input before going to complete a related independent task, requiring them to focus, shift and then refocus their attention. As with all other approaches, our decisions are based on where a child is presenting on their journey from preverbal to verbal and not whether or not they have a particular label or diagnosis, therefore attention autism is not just applicable for autistic students. Many people who adopt this approach will use different terminology to describe this intervention, such as 'bucket time' or 'bucket therapy', which then sounds more inclusive of other pupils who will also benefit from developing their attention and listening skills.

An example of how the four stages might look is illustrated below using the topic of autumn:

> Stage 1 – the bucket contains wind-up animals, for example, squirrel and hedgehog, and a fan to blow leaves – the children cannot see what is inside the bucket, and a repetitive song is used to introduce taking the lid off the bucket, for example, 'what have we got in the bucket today, bucket today, bucket today? What have we got in the bucket today? I wonder what it is . . .'
>
> Stage 2 – the stage 1 activity is then followed by making 'hot chocolate' – squirting shaving foam onto a tray, adding chocolate sprinkles, then splatting them with a spatula.
>
> Stage 3 – getting a doll ready with warm clothes that are explored and labelled. Children take turns to come and put clothes on the doll.
>
> Stage 4 – completing a leaf collage on a hedgehog outline. This is modelled by the adult leading the group before children go away and complete their own picture collage.

Symbolic Play

Symbolic play may not seem like it has an obvious link with speech, although, as speech and language therapists, we finish our training knowing that play is beneficial for language development. When we extend and expand play, we can see how the opportunities to model and rehearse new vocabulary, sentence structures and social skills emerge alongside. But when researchers have explored symbolic play in relation to speech sounds, they have found that the frequency at which a child initiates single-object symbolic play correlates to the frequency at which they initiate babble. This in turn correlates to later-emerging speech. So by seeing speech as part of a child's overall symbolic development, we can help them get started through single-object play. This might be pretending that a banana is a telephone, or perhaps using a cardboard box as a boat or a bowl as a hat. When we model this play, we are showing them that one thing can represent or stand for something else; in the same way a string of speech sounds represents or stands for something, for example, 's o ck' represents the image of a sock.

Following this early symbolic use of play with single objects and single-word language, we see 'the first milestone of symbolic play' when a child sequences two ideas together, for example, giving dolly a pretend drink, then placing her on her bed to sleep (Fein, 1981; McCune, 1995, 2010). This sequencing of play then links to sequencing longer ideas in verbal communication – in other words, building words into sentences.

Intentional Communication

At the point where communication becomes intentional, some children need additional help to send their message when they want, to another person. Many children will automatically cross over the dotted line when enough practice has taken place at the pre-intentional stage, building interaction, attention and listening skills, as well as awareness and understanding of signs and symbol. However, for some children, this is not quite enough for their verbal skills, even if they can make the jump using AAC.

PECS

PECS is not always part of the Total Speech journey, but since some children do make steps forward with their intentional communication through accessing PECS, we will offer some detail here, then signpost to further resources if this is a therapy technique you would like to learn more about. PECS is all about the exchange of one thing – usually a picture, although it can also be an object – in order to get something in return from another person. It is a bit like paying the shop keeper to get your shopping. Without this, some children appear to continue developing skills but miss the connection with others and don't manage to direct their messages successfully. Although PECS is not directly teaching verbal communication, we have worked with several children who have gone on to say their first words as a direct consequence – using the same words verbally as they have been using in symbol form. Phase 1 of PECS involves the child picking up their picture, reaching towards their communication partner and then releasing the picture into their hand before the communication partner gives them what they asked for and says the word, for example, handing them a biscuit and saying 'biscuit'. Pyramid Education is the provider of training and further education on this approach. What we have found through our clinical work is that, although PECS can take a child through to more sophisticated language use, children can tire of the exchange. For this reason, we like to explore aided language stimulation and other forms of AAC following early success with PECS.

Oral Placement Therapy

When we help a child to direct their message to another person, we often use PECS in order to teach this skill, taking them over the line from pre-intentional to intentional with their communication using pictures. This was the case in the stories of Jake, Carl and Wesley, who were introduced in Chapters 4 and 5. When it comes to speech sounds, if a child is making sounds, perhaps even saying full recognisable words, but not when it comes to communicating with others, we can use Oral Placement Therapy to help trigger the sounds intentionally. This is the case most frequently with children who have apraxia of speech. It is important to understand *why* we are using a particular method. The same tools we might use to help someone develop muscle strength can also be used to simply serve as a placement prompt for children who need this reminder of where to place their articulators. We can also use this therapy to help children achieve the correct placement for specific sounds when other methods have not worked, such as tactile input to the lips for the sounds 'm, p, b' or tactile input to the tongue tip and alveolar ridge to help placement for 'l'. Other examples are described within the previous chapter on targets.

Apraxia Shapes

These shapes are great tactile cues for developing speech in the birth-3 and preschool population predominantly but actually are perfect for any child who needs that tactile cue to help them to make lip sounds. The shapes consist of a flat triangle, square and circle to represent the sounds /p/, /m/ and /b/, as well as 3 tubes of different diameters to support lip rounding and jaw heights for vowels. The tools are also colour coded so that children who are strong visual learners can build up association between the colour and the sound as well as the shape and the sound, making use of multiple cues to achieve the target sound. The apraxia tubes are another 'go-to' for children who need extra sensory input when forming lip rounding for /oo/ (boo!) and /oh/ (go!) sounds. It's hard for children with low muscle tone and strength to pucker their lips. These tools have helped many children on our clinical caseloads to achieve these sounds beautifully. While for some, the shapes have been introduced as part of a logical next step to therapy, using our Total Speech journey outlined later in the book, other children have responded to the shapes following prolonged unsuccessful attempts at achieving sounds through other methods. They then have had break-throughs as a direct result of adding in the apraxia shapes to their routines, offering us clear clinical evidence to support their continued use.

Jolly Phonics

Jolly Phonics is an approach that has been developed for use in schools and nurseries to help children learn early letter skills, including sound-letter correspondence. Each sound is accompanied by an action and a song. As we know, movement and music are good tools for early learning, and we have seen lots of children respond positively to this approach. The songs, in particular, are short and catchy, to the point where children will continue rehearsing for a long time afterwards, making it perfect for sound practice. The actions are good for cueing children in to the different sounds, but if they need help to gain accurate placement, then you can use the Cued Articulation signs instead – this will encourage them to really watch your mouth as you model the sound and cue, rather than focus on your hands further away from your mouth. This is, of course, not the only early phonics approach available, so other schemes that also teach these skills would also be useful. We find that early phonics knowledge improves awareness of sounds for speech, and when children are able to recognise letters, they gain a valuable visual support as well. When children can read out loud, they often have improved clarity than when they are speaking without reading.

Cued Articulation

Cued Articulation has been discussed in Chapter 3, and it is a really simple way of adding visual cues to speech that also encourage children to make their own cues as they imitate; this helps with motor planning as well as offering a tactile prompt on their own mouths. These cues are preferable to the kind used in Jolly Phonics, as they all centre around the mouth and relate to the physical production of speech. If a child is watching you make the cues, they will likely be looking at your mouth, whereas when you are doing a Jolly Phonics action, they will miss out on any visual clues from your mouth as you speak. As with other visual or tactile prompts, they can be faded out as a child makes progress, to the point where only verbal input is required.

Word Flips Book – CV Productions

When single sounds are emerging and becoming more intentional, working on CV productions comes next. In fact, some speech and language professionals prefer to begin at this level as the smallest speech unit, arguing that words are never produced with just a single sound. CV combinations allow them to begin working on the movement between sounds, such as in the DTTC approach, right from the start. We have used a book called *Word Flips*, which contains many CV words, each repeated 3 times in a row, for example, pie, pie, pie, and the individual words can then be flipped over so that you can create 3 CV words that are different, for example, pie, pea, pay, as a step up in difficulty. The words can also be lined up so that you can keep the vowel the same but change the consonant, for example, pea, tea, key.

Video Modelling

Video modelling is a way of teaching new skills through video footage. Taking advantage of a child's interest in screens, as well as observations that some children will start to copy behaviours that they see on screen rather than an adult physically in front of them, we can use video modelling to help teach speech as well as other skills they may need to learn. For example, by watching another child have a haircut, this might lead to them tolerating a haircut because they are prepared for what to expect; watching 2 children playing a turn-taking game can teach the rules and expectations in preparation for playing the same game with another child in school; watching videos of someone saying speech sounds – particularly if the videos focus on the mouth area – can lead to a child attempting to imitate speech sounds. The person in the video can make a big difference. You might not be able to record Thomas the Tank Engine or Rapunzel modelling speech sounds; however, a favourite adult, family member or peer could be a reason for some children to want to watch the videos and try to copy the sounds. There is an approach called Gemiini, which has video modelling at its core. It is aimed at home use with minimal additional time and effort required for a child to follow its programme. The idea is that through repeatedly watching the video content, which shows speech production close up, with words then placed into context, a child will build up enough exposure and repetitions to then start imitating. With the recent growth of telehealth (online speech and language therapy), it is perhaps more relevant now than before as much of the speech and language therapy profession has at least partially, if not completely, spent some time over the past 2–3 years developing online/virtual support when in-person therapy sessions have not been possible. Gemiini has built up a large database of testimonials crediting the approach with their child's success. In our experience, where a child has delayed speech and expressive language skills, perhaps associated with autism or Down syndrome, but has the ability to imitate across a range of other areas, video modelling has proven very beneficial as a tool in the speech toolkit. However, where a child has additional physical or motor challenges, they may struggle to imitate from video input alone, and may still require additional tactile supports; for example, a child with apraxia of speech might not respond so readily to this approach on its own. The concept of video modelling is one which features in many different areas of communication therapy, such as play and social interaction. We might encourage a parent or caregiver to video their own interaction and play with their child to then view back and analyse. Video content in storytelling and support for expressive language or narrative skills is valuable, such as in the use of personalised video books. If you take a 'first words' book, where pictures of early vocabulary feature one picture per page, but prepare this in video format, you are adding an extra route in to learning, one which allows for a child to really tune in to the mouth movements. When sharing a physical picture book, it is likely that the child's attention is on the picture, so they will miss out on the visual mouth cues as you say the word, whereas a video production of the word as you hold up the picture to the side of your mouth will help to promote focus on the mouth.

Nuffield Dyspraxia Programme

The Nuffield Dyspraxia Programme (NDP) was first published in 1985 in the UK to support children with verbal dyspraxia and other speech sound disorders. It remains a popular resource and has a good evidence base to back up its usage. Although its name clearly makes it the go-to for working with verbal dyspraxia, it is also beneficial for children with other clinical needs due to its design and structure. The programme takes you through a clear small-steps progression from single sounds through to sentences one stage at a time. It has appealed to many of our visual learners as well as those who like familiarity and predictability – perfect for the autistic pupils we have supported with a range of speech needs. Due to the small-steps progression and repetition of material, it also lends itself well to children with learning difficulties. We have found success with children who have Down syndrome who have taken to the visual materials and used their reading skills to access the programme and support their speech using their areas of strength. We also like to use the framework of the programme but adapted to the way children like or need to learn. For example, if we have a child in the group who loves cartoon characters, then we can feed in the sounds and words at the right levels but use cartoon character names and references instead of the words from the programme sheets. We can also feed the practice and repetition to play and games rather than sitting at a table with worksheets. So when we hear someone say, "Oh, but my child is too young to start the Nuffield Programme" or "They won't engage with all the worksheets", it is ok to get creative and still support their speech sound development.

AAC

When children start speaking, they have heard people speaking around them for a long time, they have heard multiple repetitions of words and they have had time to learn and rehearse before gaining the confidence to start speaking.

The first 'A' in AAC stands for augmentative communication. When you augment something, you add to it or supplement. Augmentative communication is when you add something to your speech (e.g. sign language, pictures, a letter board). This can make your message clearer to your listener.

The second 'A' in AAC stands for alternative communication. This is when you are not able to speak. It is also when your speech is not understood by others. In this case, you need a different way to communicate.

Essentially AAC can be tools, systems, devices or strategies which would seek to give a person the maximum opportunity to communicate when they cannot rely on speech.

This can be as simple as signing or symbols, and in particular, they often have not had the exposure to signing and symbols from people around them prior to the decision to teach them the method or methods. For this reason, at the pre-intentional level of communication, we recommend that adults begin modelling signs and symbols as early as possible so that if they get to the point where they need to use these methods expressively, they have a better chance of being able to do so effectively as they have already been taught in this way. Sometimes people think about technology when they hear 'AAC', but it includes many no-tech or low-tech options. It is these no- or low-tech options that we would begin with, such as having symbols in the environment to label or be shown when introducing key activities. Signs can be used during everyday routines. We can also begin modelling the use of core words (as discussed in the targets chapter earlier in the book). These low-tech options then become natural opportunities to use when the child develops intentional communication before speech. As they begin using and develop early skills in using low-tech options, you can monitor whether this leads to speech – as it does for many children – or if speech is still further along their journey, then it is a good idea to begin modelling higher-tech options such as symbol based communication apps. Again, through modelling, you are helping the children to see how it works before they are expected to use it themselves.

At this point, we would like to discuss the benefits of having access to AAC well into a verbal communication journey. While AAC may begin as a completely alternative method of communication for a child, as their speech skills develop, they may benefit from access to AAC as an additional tool for many reasons. First of all, AAC may allow a child to express themselves in longer, more complex sentences; it may aid the access of specific vocabulary; it may also help with intelligibility as a 'backup' device when not understood; or it may be a less demanding communication method if they are tired or anxious. The auditory reinforcement that AAC can provide is also not only priceless but independence building – which is every parent's dream for their child. We also know that AAC is not something that will prevent children from talking or trying so hard to use their voice. Quite the opposite, in fact – we have seen many children's speech develop as a result of their AAC use.

Technology Speech Sound Apps

As any parent, caregiver or teacher will tell you, the level of engagement that can be achieved when a child is given an iPad can significantly improve.

When speech exercises have sometimes become challenging or less interesting to a child, a speech sound app can be a great tool to introduce, which may give another level to practice. As we know, the more practice we can achieve, the more likely we are to improve outcomes.

We also only have to refer back to our communication pyramid on page 16 to remind ourselves that 'attention and listening' underpins a child's progress through the levels: comprehension, expression and, lastly, speech sounds. It is therefore also logical to expect that if we have achieved 'attention and listening', then we are more likely to therefore progress through these levels.

The number of speech sound apps that are now available is significant; however, in our experience, there are some that have been tried and tested and can be extremely effective for improving speech sound awareness and production.

The following list is not definitive in any way, shape or form but are merely some of our favourites:

Apps for Speech Therapy

Table 8.1 Apps for speech

Name of the app	Brief description of how it works and what you can do with it	What does it target
Speech Tutor	This app has a side view and front view animated videos of how the tongue makes sounds in the mouth. It covers the following sounds: p, b, t, d, k, g, n, m, ing, f, v, s, z, sh, ch, j, l, r and th. There is a written description of each sound, and you can also record your own attempt too.	Single sounds
Articulation Station	This is a fantastic app where you choose words with targeted sounds at the beginning, medial or final position in a word. The free version gives you just the sound 'p', so you need to purchase other sounds if you want to cover others. There are photo pictures and some American English included. There is the option to delete American pictures. Sentences and stories are also available with targeted sounds within them, which is great for bombardment activities. You can, lastly, record your child saying a particular word and then play it back.	Words with chosen sounds at beginning, medial, final. p, b, m, h, w, y, d, n, t, k, g, ing, f, v, ch, j, l, r, s, z, sh, th. Matching pairs game or flashcards game.
Tiga Talk Campfire Adventure	Interactive storybook which allows children to develop speech sounds through voice-controlled interactions.	It covers Core 19 phonetic sounds

(Continued)

Table 8.1 (Continued)

Name of the app	Brief description of how it works and what you can do with it	What does it target
Minimal Pairs	There is a free version which mostly just encompasses s blends. The full version aims to tackle commonly used phonological processes such as final consonant deletion, fronting, cluster reduction, stopping, voicing and gliding. You can record your child saying a particular word and then play it back. It helps with auditory discrimination skills, contrast drills and repetition drills, amongst other skills.	Minimal pairs pictures for children of different ages (based on American age bands). Animation pictures, not photos.
Bubble	A very simple app that does exactly what it says. A great way to practice those early lip sounds: b, p and m. There is a bubble on the screen that pops when touched.	Could focus on word 'pop', 'bubble', 'more'.
Boo Articulation	This is an app with a cute little frog that produces the target sounds. There is a lite and full version. You are able to assemble your own variations by putting the consonant plus the vowel, so this is great way to target the CV and VC level of speech sound practice.	All consonants are available on the full version, with the different vowels possible.
Speech Pairs	Another minimal pairs game that will target those common phonological processes. Essentially the child hears the words and can then record themselves saying the word. There is a view of an animated tongue position for the word visual info. Lastly, you are able to keep a record of how the child is doing too.	Minimal pairs pictures for children of different ages (based on American age bands).
Artikpik	This app consists of flashcard cartoon pictures for each sound in single words and also in sentences.	Free version – th, w, y and h.

Name of the app	Brief description of how it works and what you can do with it	What does it target
	There are options to play a matching game and also just look at flashcards. Again you can record your own attempt at a word and playback for further feedback.	Paid version – p, b, m, n, t, d, j, f, v, ch, sh, k, g, s, z, l, r and blends, and you can create your own decks.
		American voice. YouTube demo.
Minimal Pair Pack Therapy Box	A huge bank of 700 drawings of words used for minimal pairs initial word position. This can be a great investment of resources due to the amount available.	P, b, m, n, t, d, k, g, f, v, s, z, j, y, w, r, l, th, sh, ch.
	It helps with auditory discrimination skills, contrast drills and repetition drills, amongst other skills.	
Artic Castle Webber Photo Super Duper Publications	Choose a sound, choose the position in the word, number of syllables and word level. Full version has 3000 photo words covering 24 phonemes.	Speech production; set it up for each child with a specific goal. Hear the word and then record the child's attempt.
	3 activities.	
	Photo fun – look and say word	
	Arcade games – tap object, then picture appears, say it and score a point.	
	Matching – 6/10 pics to match.	
Big Mouth Sound Pack	Using the big mouth programme and characters, child makes the sound related to the characters. Child can listen to stories related to a big mouth sound.	Sound production
Starfall ABCs	This app is an excellent tool for helping your child learn the alphabet and practice their sounds.	

(*Continued*)

Table 8.1 (Continued)

Name of the app	Brief description of how it works and what you can do with it	What does it target
My Talking Tom	This app is always a popular one and features a cat that repeats everything you say back to you in a funny voice, and children love it. It works really well for motivating children to practice their sounds and words. You can challenge them to see how many times they can get the cat to say the 'p' or the 'sh' sound correctly. As a reward, they can then access the game's other features, which include feeding, dressing, and petting Tom.	Whatever the child or adults decides to say!

On a final note, these apps cannot replace the benefits and skills of a trained professional or committed parent who is prepared to support a child with their speech sound development, but it can add another layer of fun and motivation.

Conclusions

Our goal in writing this book has been to add fresh information based on clinical insight in a field that is lacking in empirical guidance. Through exploring the theory and then applying it to real-life cases, we have developed a clear need to draw on many different theories, to integrate theory with such areas as sensory profiles, learning styles and physical conditions; to be flexible in our clinical decision-making so that we really do take into account the children and young people's views as well as the many supporting and sometimes competing needs within wider development, including priorities within school settings or home dynamics. We have endeavoured to draw on key themes to shed light and clarity on what can become a very complex line of work – supporting speech clarity in children and young people with complex learning and neurological differences. By critically appraising the literature, taking time to really get to know and understand each child or young person as an individual and incorporating goals that align with their motivations and desires as future communicators, we have seen many successful stories where children with 'challenging' or 'complex' needs have achieved real progress with speech, often against the odds and nearly always through an abundance of determination, especially in the early days. We hope that by sharing this with you as a reader, you will be feeling more confident in your own clinical work, give yourself permission to take the time to adapt and be flexible with your therapeutic approaches, understand the importance of practice-based evidence as well as evidence-based practice and continue with a positive outlook on behalf of all of your clients.

Meet the Total Speech graduates . . .

Elliot's Story

Karen met Elliot when was 3 years old, an inquisitive little boy with a love of numbers and letters. He would run to greet everyone who entered the classroom, and he loved to initiate interactions with people around school. Elliot soon responded to the approaches used to support pre-intentional communicators, and he crossed the dotted line to intentional communication by signing some core words and using PECS. He was able to use very few sounds, all in his play, babble and when communicating, and had just one word used with clear purpose – 'Mama'. For a long time, Elliot accessed Oral Placement Therapy with the goal of expanding his speech sound repertoire, but he wasn't ready to respond; instead, he continued to make excellent progress with AAC, and when he began using his own high-tech communication app, he was capable of holding a conversation on a variety of topics. Then, sometime after using the app, Elliot was heard trying to speak alongside the app, as well as being an enthusiastic member of phonics lessons. He was finally ready to use his voice, and so, with his AAC fully established, he worked hard to go from the very beginning of the Nuffield Dyspraxia Programme all the way to the end, where he can be found refining his speech clarity in full sentences at age 10. If you meet Elliot, you meet the most fabulous communicator, who greets every person with such infectious enthusiasm, and before you know it, you will be in the middle of a full-blown conversation and friends for life! Elliot is a reminder for us all how we should expect speech from all children who clearly want to express themselves, no matter how long it takes for them to get started and no matter whether they are doing well with an alternative system – because for all the incredible technological advancements, no app can fully replace a child's own voice.

Harry's Story

Harry followed a similar journey to Elliot, but we didn't get to meet him until he was 8 years old. At this point Harry had already reached the point of using a high-tech communication app but was clearly wanting to use his voice as well. His speech attempts consisted of vowels but no consonants. He used the correct vowel sounds for the words he used, which meant that sometimes you could work out what he was saying, enough to know that he had definite ideas and messages to send, but his mouth wasn't translating his thoughts clearly enough. Harry had a severe case of verbal dyspraxia, but for years, those working with him attributed his speech difficulties to his autism diagnosis. As a result, the dyspraxia went unrecognised, and he did not receive any support to develop his speech skills. When his situation changed for the better, with lots of support and encouragement, Harry began to make progress first with Oral Placement Therapy and Cued Articulation, then he started to work through the stages of the Nuffield Dyspraxia Programme. He is so proud when he manages to successfully communicate verbally with others, and the smile on his face says it all. Harry does still have a long way to go on his verbal journey, so the close support of his mother, therapy team and school staff are crucial to keep momentum and encourage Harry to keep working hard on his speech daily, especially when he finds it difficult.

Eleanor's Story

When Eleanor was 3 years old, she was completely non-verbal, she spent her nursery days spinning in circles and did not appear to pay much attention to either the people or the activities in the room. She appeared to be a happy little girl, but it was difficult to build any connection with her. All of her needs were anticipated by others as it was difficult to identify any intentional messages she might be sending. Eleanor was joined by others using Intensive Interaction and gradually moved from Encounter through to Awareness level. She was supported hand over hand to take part in Wake up Shake up sessions. During attention autism, she was initially on the periphery of the room, but in time she began to take notice and hover nearby to observe and eventually anticipate what was coming out of the bucket. No one who worked with Eleanor at the time could have predicted the change that was to come. But with the consistent efforts of the team around her, Eleanor began to slowly but surely make communication gains.

Her play began to evolve so that she was exploring more toys. Teaching staff would sit with her, commenting and labelling her play with pictures as she was exposed to low-tech AAC. Eleanor was in a class with other early communicators, and as she improved in awareness of others, she began to pick up on how the other children were communicating. She would imitate her peers picking up pictures to request their favourite toys and snacks, and she began to also copy her signing peers as they asked for 'more' and 'stop' during music lessons. Finally, Eleanor realised she could copy verbal language to great rewards. Before anyone had paused long enough to implement an alternative communication system with Eleanor, she crossed over the line from pre-intentional to intentional communication with confidence. Eleanor became as verbal as anyone could ever have wished for, in the space of just 6 months!

When we are met with children like Elliot, Harry and Eleanor, it is easy to see how the decisions we make as clinicians can have a clear impact on the trajectory of their communication development. Taking their skills at face value during the initial meeting could invite a conservative take on their chances of becoming verbal communicators. We might focus a great deal of our time developing early interaction skills without beginning to look ahead at function communication, language and speech. We might spend time in conversations using words like 'basic', 'early stages', 'non-verbal' and look for alternative means of communication as a way of propping up communication skills in the absence of speech but with an assumption that it is likely to be a long-term solution. If others challenge those thoughts, ideas and actions, we can decide that they are 'unrealistic' or 'too aspirational'. Suggestions of goals relating to speech or developing verbal skills could be met with unsuccessful attempts at mapping on some of the traditional approaches described in Chapter 3 with auditory and visual input.

Set the Bar High

In essence, what we have done to help these 3 children succeed – as with many, many others over the years – is to flip the narrative to positive, encouraging and optimistic goals. We have expected them to reach the point of being successful verbal communicators, and we have supported yet challenged them to get there at every step along the way. We have also recognised the need to join up our work with other key team members from home and school, to problem solve together, to bring in what we know about physical, medical or cognitive skills and needs. Sometimes our role has been 'motivator' or 'cheerleader' to keep the momentum going when therapy is painstakingly slow and people are tempted to give up. But the view from the top, when a child says their first word, is one of the most rewarding. We have access to an abundance of tools for speech, language and communication development, and we have no reason to limit the number of tools we use and blend together when children need them. Our Total Speech kit is full to overflowing, and we know that there will be more techniques and therapy approaches from pioneering colleagues to add in the future.

The Total Speech Journey

How children and young people move through the graphic we have created can vary. Sometimes they will access all the approaches in a neat order, moving from left to right at a steady rate, increasing verbal skills as AAC is needed less and less frequently; other times they move more quickly through the stages of AAC before they can tap into their intentional verbal skills. We have supported children and young people of all ages, from 2 to 18, and found that our toolkit of approaches has been able to adapt to the different ages. If you would like help in doing this, please do reach out and contact us, and we would love to support your further. Perhaps we should also add that when it comes to speech production, we might need to dig deep into our toolkits until we find the right match of techniques and approaches for some children; this is due to the many different classifications of speech sound disorders. A child might have difficulties in multiple areas of the Stackhouse and Wells speech model (discussed in Chapter 3), and they might benefit from therapy that covers auditory, visual and tactile input. Finally, we are acutely aware of our focus on children and young people as opposed to adults. This is reflective of our clinical backgrounds and experience and is in no way intended to imply that the methods covered could not be useful in helping adults to also develop their speech skills. With what we now know about brain plasticity, we are confident that many adults could be just a few steps away from developing their verbal communication skills given the right support and encouragement.

Bibliography

ASHA. (2023). https://www.asha.org/practice-portal/clinical-topics/articulation-and-phonology/

Boyd, A., Golding, J., Macleod, J., Lawlor, D. A., Fraser, A., Henderson, J., Molloy, L., Ness, A., Ring, S., & Davey Smith, G. (2013). Cohort profile: The 'children of the 90s' – the index offspring of the Avon Longitudinal Study of parents and children. *International Journal of Epidemiology, 42*(1), 111–127. http://doi.org/10.1093/ije/dys064

Broomfield, J., & Dodd, B. (2004). Children with speech and language disability: Caseload characteristics. *International Journal of Language & Communication Disorders, 39*(3), 303–324.

Cambridge Dictionary. (2023). https://dictionary.cambridge.org/dictionary/english/articulation

Dell. (2000). https://pubmed.ncbi.nlm.nih.gov/11185769/

Dell, G. S., Reed, K. D., Adams, D. R., & Meyer, A. S. (2000). Speech errors, phonotactic constraints, and implicit learning: A study of the role of experience in language production. *Journal of Experimental Psychology: Learning, Memory, and Cognition, 26*(6), 1355–1367.

DeLoache, J. S. (2002). Early development of the understanding and use of symbolic artifacts. In U. Goswami (Ed.), *Blackwell handbook of childhood cognitive development* (pp. 206–226). Blackwell Publishing.

Dodd, B., Holm, A., Hua, Z., & Crosbie, S. (2003). Phonological development: A normative study of British English-speaking children. *Clinical Linguistics and Phonetics, 17*(8), 617–643.

Fein, G. G. (1981). Pretend play in childhood: An integrative review. *Child Development, 52*, 1095–1118. https://doi.org/10.2307/1129497 https://core.ac.uk/download/pdf/82771702.pdf

https://educalingo.com/en/dic-en/phonotactic

https://pubs.asha.org/doi/10.1044/2015_JSLHR-S-14-0282

James, D. G. H. (2001). The use of phonological processes in Australian children aged 2 to 7:11 years. *Advances in Speech-Language Pathology, 3*, 109–128.

McCune, L. (1995, 2010). A normative study of representational play in the transition to language. *Developmental Psychology, 31*(2), 198–206.

McLeod, S., Harrison, L., & McCormack, J. (2012). The intelligibility in context scale: Validity and reliability of a subjective rating measure. *Journal of Speech, Language and Hearing Research, 55*(2), 648–656. http://doi.org/10.1044/1092-4388(2011/10-0130)

Nathan, L., Stackhouse, J., Goulandris, N., & Snowling, M. J. (2004). The development of early literacy skills among children with speech difficulties: A test of the "critical age hypothesis". *Journal of Speech, Language, and Hearing Research, 47*(2), 377–391. http://doi.org/10.1044/1092-4388(2004/031)

NHS England. (2013) https://www.england.nhs.uk/tis/wp-content/uploads/sites/17/2014/09/tis-guide-finding-the-evidence-07nov.pdf

Passy, J. (2010). *Cued articulation – consonants and vowels.* ACER Press.

Phonotactics. (2023). https://educalingo.com/en/dic-en/phonotactics

Pring, T., Flood, E., Dodd, B., & Joffe, V. (2012). The working practices and clinical experiences of paediatric speech and language therapists: A national UK survey. *International Journal of Language & Communication Disorders, 47*(6), 696–708. http://doi.org/10.1111/j.1460-6984.2012.00177.x

RCSLT. (2023). https://www.rcslt.org/speech-and-language-therapy/clinical-information/speech-sound-disorders/#section-3

Rosenfeld-Johnson, S. (2009). *Oral placement therapy for speech clarity and feeding* (rev. 4th ed.). Innovative Therapists International.

Shriberg, L. D., Austin, D., Lewis, B. A., McSweeny, J. L., & Wilson, D. L. (1997). The Speech Disorders Classification System (SDCS): Extensions and lifespan reference data. *Journal of Speech, Language, and Hearing Research, 40*, 723–740.

Smit, A. B. (1993a). Phonologic error distributions in the Iowa-Nebraska articulation norms project: Consonant singletons. *Journal of Speech and Hearing Research, 36*, 533–547.

Smit, A. B. (1993b). Phonologic error distributions in the Iowa-Nebraska articulation norms project: Word-initial consonant clusters. *Journal of Speech and Hearing Research, 36*, 931–947.

Smith, L. B., & Jones, S. S. (2011). Symbolic play connects to language through visual object recognition. *Developmental Science, 14*(5), 1142–1149.

Stackhouse, J., & Wells, B. (1997). *Children's speech and literacy difficulties I: A psycholinguistic framework.* Whurr Publishers.

Templin, M. C. (1957). *Certain language skills in children: Their development and interrelationships.* University of Minnesota Press.

Wikipedia. (2023). https://en.wikipedia.org/wiki/Perception#:~:text=Perception%20 (from%20Latin%20perceptio%20'gathering,the%20presented%20 information%20or%20environment

www.hanen.org/Helpful-Info/Articles/Imitation-with-Children-on-the-Autism-Spectrum.aspx

Appendices

Table A.1 Ideas for sound work relating to labiodental, alveolar and velar placements

Word Structure/Placement	Labiodental	Alveolar	Velar
Single Sound	/f/ /v/	/n/ /t/ /d/ /l/	/k/ /g/
CV/VC	far, four, oof!	no, toe, day, lie on, eat, add, ill	car, go, key, ark, egg
CVCV	coffee, funny, favour, never	nanny, teddy, dirty, dinner, dolly, leader	cooker, bigger, colour, goggles
CVC	Have, wave, Cough, laugh	dot, lid, doll, nod, bed, bell	cake, knock, bag, game
Phrases	fee fi fo fum! turn it off	It's not . . . mine/yours/ big etc.	What's in the bag? Ready, steady, go!

Table A.2 Template for planning your Total Speech group

Group goals 1. 2. 3.
Resources needed:
Warm-up Song: Hello: Group rules:
Sound awareness activities Listening game: Matching sounds: Selecting sounds:
Placement awareness activities Jaw activities: Lips activities: Tongue activities:
Sound production Activities:
Word productions Activities:
Functional game:

Appendix 3 – My Sound Book Template

My /b/ Sound Book (substitute /b/ for the relevant sound)
Page 1: things I have found around school that begin with /b/ *E.g. ball, bag*
Page 2: words I have found in my reading book beginning with /b/ *E.g. be, but*
Page 3: things I have found at home that begin with /b/ *E.g. biscuit, banana*
Page 4: more /b/ words – stick pictures of /b/ words here!

Index

Note: page numbers in *italics* indicate a figure and page numbers in **bold** indicate a table.